UNEP
United Nations Environment Programme

Integrated Policymaking for Sustainable Development

A reference manual

August 2009

Acknowledgements

This manual was prepared by Scott Fritzen, Michael Howlett, M. Ramesh, and Wu Xun of the Lee Kuan Yew School of Public Policy, National University of Singapore and Fulai Sheng of the United Nations Environment Programme (UNEP) under the supervision of Hussein Abaza, Chief of UNEP's Economics and Trade Branch. Apart from authoring the introductory and closing chapters, Sheng Fulai also provided substantive editing to the entire manual and managed the production of the manual from inception to publication. Rory Canwell of McGill University provided illustrative examples of climate change to accompany the chapters that describe the various stages of integrated policymaking. He also provided editorial support.

This manual has benefited from guidance generously provided by Nicholas Bonvoisin of the United Nations Economic Commission for Europe, Jiri Dusik of the Regional Environmental Center for Central and Eastern Europe, Jan Joost Kessler of AIDEnvironment, Maria Partidário (IST – Instituto Superior Tecnico), Rob Verheem of the Netherlands' Commission for Environmental Impact Assessment.

Valuable inputs were also provided by Kulsum Ahmed and Fernando Loayza of the World Bank, Dieudonné Bitondo of the University of Dschang in Cameroon, Claire Brown of the UNEP-World Conservation Monitoring Centre, Peter Croal of the Canadian International Development Agency, Mark Curtis and Rory Canwell of McGill University, Barry Dalal-Clayton of International Institute for Environment and Development, Clive Gorge of the University of Manchester, Linda Ghanime of the United Nations Development Programme (UNDP) and the Secretariat of the Convention for Biological Diversity (SCBD), John Hobbery of UNEP-UNDP Poverty Environment Initiative, Jean Hugé of Vrije Universiteit Brussel, Remy Paris and Candice Stevens of the Organization for Economic Co-operation and Development (OECD), Bobbi Schijf of the Netherlands' Commission for Environmental Impact Assessment, John D. Shilling of the Millennium Institute, and independent experts Barry Sadler, Salah El Serafy, and Matthew Stilwell.

Thanks also to the participants at number of consultative meetings held between 2005 and 2007 which helped shape this manual. These meetings and related communication processes were supported by UNEP staff members including Desiree Leon, Rahila Mughal, and Karim Ouahidi as well as UNEP consultants and interns including Louise Gallagher, Cristina Gueco, Chloe Hill, Nazlee Khalis, Ngan Tim Lam, Veronique Marx, Katharina Peschen, Andrea Smith, Miroslava Tsolova, and Bin You.

Several UNEP staff members also provided substantive inputs. They include: Benjamin Simmons, Anja von Moltke, Asad Naqvi, Fatma Ben Fadhl, Maria Cecilia Pineda, Cornelia Iliescu and Vera Weick.

United Nations Environment Programme

The United Nations Environment Programme (UNEP) is the overall coordinating environmental organization of the United Nations system. Its mission is to provide leadership and encourage partnerships in caring for the environment by inspiring, informing and enabling nations and people to improve their quality of life without compromising that of future generations. In accordance with its mandate, UNEP works to observe, monitor and assess the state of the global environment, improve the scientific understanding of how environmental change occurs, and in turn, how such change can be managed by action-oriented national policies and international agreements. UNEP's capacity building work thus centers on helping countries strengthen environmental management in diverse areas that include freshwater and land resource management, the conservation and sustainable use of biodiversity, marine and coastal ecosystem management, and cleaner industrial production and eco-efficiency, among many others.

UNEP, which is headquartered in Nairobi, Kenya, marked its first 35 years of service in 2007. During this time, in partnership with a global array of collaborating organizations, UNEP has achieved major advances in the development of international environmental policy and law, environmental monitoring and assessment, and the understanding of the science of global change. This work also supports the successful development and implementation of the world's major environmental conventions. In parallel, UNEP administers several multilateral environmental agreements (MEAs) including the Vienna Convention's Montreal Protocol on Substances that Deplete the Ozone Layer, the Convention on International Trade in Endangered Species of Wild Fauna and Flora (CITES), the Basel Convention on the Control of Transboundary Movements of Hazardous Wastes and their Disposal (SBC), the Convention on Prior Informed Consent Procedure for Certain Hazardous Chemicals and Pesticides in International Trade (Rotterdam Convention, PIC) and the Cartagena Protocol on Biosafety to the Convention on Biological Diversity as well as the Stockholm Convention on Persistent Organic Pollutants (POPs).

Division of Technology, Industry and Economics

The mission of the Division of Technology, Industry and Economics (DTIE) is to encourage decision makers in government, local authorities and industry to develop and adopt policies, strategies and practices that are cleaner and safer, make efficient use of natural resources, ensure environmentally sound management of chemicals, and reduce pollution and risks for humans and the environment. In addition, it seeks to enable implementation of conventions and international agreements and encourage the internalization of environmental costs. UNEP DTIE's strategy in carrying out these objectives is to influence decision-making through partnerships with other international organizations, governmental authorities, business and industry, and non-governmental organizations; facilitate knowledge management through networks; support implementation of conventions; and work closely with UNEP regional offices. The Division, with its Director and Division Office in Paris, consists of one centre and five branches located in Paris, Geneva and Osaka.

Economics and Trade Branch

The Economics and Trade Branch (ETB) is one of the five branches of DTIE. ETB seeks to support a transition to a green economy by enhancing the capacity of governments, businesses and civil society to integrate environmental considerations in economic, trade, and financial policies and practices. In so doing, ETB focuses its activities on:

1. Stimulating investment in green economic sectors;

2. Promoting integrated policy assessment and design;

3. Strengthening environmental management through subsidy reform;

4. Promoting mutually supportive trade and environment policies; and

5. Enhancing the role of the financial sector in sustainable development.

Over the last decade, ETB has been a leader in the area of economic and trade policy assessment through its projects and activities focused on building national capacities to undertake integrated assessments – a process for analyzing the economic, environmental and social effects of current and future policies, examining the linkages between these effects, and formulating policy response packages and measures aimed at promoting sustainable development. This work has provided countries with the necessary information and analysis to limit and mitigate negative consequences from economic and trade policies and to enhance positive effects. The assessment techniques and tools developed over the years are now being applied to assist countries in transitioning towards a green economy.

■ For more information on the general programme of the Economics and Trade Branch, please contact:

Hussein Abaza

Chief, Economics and Trade Branch (ETB)

Division of Technology,

Industry and Economics (DTIE)

United Nations Environment Programme (UNEP)

11-13 Chemin des Anemones

1219 Chatelaine/Geneva

Tel : +41-22-917 81 79

Fax :+41-22-917 80 76

http://www.unep.ch/etb

Contents

Foreword

Most of the problems facing the world today – from financial crisis to climate change – result directly from human activities.

Questionable lending and borrowing activities in the housing market, reinforced by significant shortcomings of sophisticated financing tools in large part, sewed the seeds years ago for the prevailing financial and then economic crisis. Excessive burning of fossil fuels to power the global economy allied to unsustainable land use is triggering and accelerating climate change.

These activities do not take place in a vacuum; they are conditioned not only by norms and habits, but also to a significant extent by public policies – rules, regulations, interest rates, taxes, subsidies, to name but a few. For example the more than US$200 billion annual subsidy for the production and consumption of fossil fuels plays its part in perpetuating their inefficient use and our dependency on carbon.

Indeed, the failure to consider system-wide implications of policies – including the lack of policies or lack of effective policy enforcement – is a major driver behind many of the problems facing governments today.

An integrated approach to policymaking, the theme of this manual, will assist policymakers to avoid solving one problem while creating another. It will also contribute to a society's multiple objectives – including social, economic and environmental ones.

This is one of the key messages and central aims of UNEP's Global Green New Deal. The "deal" takes its departure from the notion that the US$3 trillion-worth of stimulus packages engaged to combat the global economic meltdown can deal with current and future crises – from climate change and unemployment to natural resource scarcity – if wisely and creatively targeted.

Indeed the policy choices and market signals made now and over the coming months and years will determine whether the stage can be set for a resource efficient, low carbon, decent job-generating and poverty-cutting Green Economy for the 21st century.

This manual draws on the decades-long experience of UNEP and other organizations in the field of sustainability-motivated policy assessment as well as recent advances in public policy science.

The approach described in the manual places sustainability considerations and policy assessment within the overall policymaking cycle, thereby making sustainability an integral part — rather than an "add-on" — to any such process.

The manual suggests using sustainable development as a major filter for prioritizing competing issues and for formulating and deciding on policy choices while emphasizing a culture of learning, monitoring and evaluation alongside involving stakeholders and managing their dynamics at every stage.

I hope that this manual will prove useful and indeed inspiring to policymakers and analysts, not only in the environmental community, but also in economic and social spheres and that it can play a role in realizing a more intelligent management of human, financial and natural capital.

I see this manual as a bridge that can potentially connect our various policy communities in our common pursuit of sustainable development and for delivering tomorrow's economy, today.

Achim Steiner

UN Under-Secretary General and Executive Director, United Nations Environment Programme

Executive summary

This reference manual provides guidance on Integrated Policymaking (IP) with a view to promoting Sustainable Development (SD) in its environmental, social, and economic (ESE) dimensions. IP:

- is proposed as a normative policymaking approach that considers critical ESE implications and interactions associated with policy issues and their potential solutions;

- places solutions within a policy cycle in order to ensure that policy issues are appropriately defined, potential solutions compared, the solution that increases synergies and reduces trade-offs adopted, and the adopted solution implemented, monitored, and evaluated;

- aligns policy development with the political, institutional, and analytical realities of the policy environment.

This summary is prepared to enable senior policy and decision makers to appreciate IP's added value. The full report is available for practitioners who are convinced of the need for SD and seeking guidance on how to make public policies contribute to it.

The need for an integrated approach to policymaking has been expressed in major international processes such as the Millennium Development Goals (MDGs), the World Summit on Sustainable Development (WSSD), and the Millennium Ecosystem Assessment (MA). In addition, a number of Multilateral Environmental Agreements (MEAs) such as the Convention on Biological Diversity (CBD) and the United Nations Framework Convention on Climate Change (UNFCCC) have included clauses that require policy integration.

A number of institutions including the Organization of Economic Co-operation and Development's Development Assistance Committee (OECD DAC), the United Nations Economic Commission for Europe (UNECE), the World Bank, the European Commission (EC), and UNEP have responded to these calls for policy integration by promoting various sustainability-oriented assessments of public policies, programmes and plans.

The IP process proposed in this manual builds on the assessment efforts thus far and provides another response to the need for a proactive approach to integrating SD into policymaking. IP:

- locks SD considerations into a policy process from the beginning, before a policy issue is even brought onto the government agenda and certainly before any policy proposal is put on the table;

- internalizes sustainability-oriented assessment without identifying it separately so as to make such assessment a natural and integral component of the policy process.

IP – in its most intuitive sense of considering diverse factors when making policies – is important for at least three reasons:

1. A policy that addresses one issue can affect other issues, which may not be less important. For example, inappropriate biofuel subsidies to reduce reliance on fossil fuels can contribute to food shortage and deforestation.

2. Synergies among different issues exist and a policy intervention can be designed to achieve multiple benefits. For example, investing in basic health care not only contributes to poverty reduction, but also raises labour productivity.

3. Successful implementation of a policy relies on the support from a range of stakeholders who may have diverse values and interests that need to be harmonized. For example, imposing anti-dumping duties on low-price imports may help protect domestic producers but is also likely to hurt importers, retailers, and low-income consumers at home.

This summary is expected to motivate its audience to adopt an integrated approach to policymaking and use this manual. The rest of the summary will highlight key elements of such an approach, starting from a conceptual framework of sustainable development and moving on to reflecting such a framework at major stages of a policy cycle.

It should be noted that policymaking is not typically a linear process. Different policy participants may also enter into a policy process at its different stages deploying different "building blocks" of analytical and process-related tools.

The "building blocks" concept connects the IPSD manual with the *Integrated Assessment: Mainstreaming Sustainability into Policymaking.* The Guidance details the use of building blocks in the IA process and highlights the connections with a six-steps policy cycle that considers policy analysis a separate stage in the process, an approach more suitable for IA purposes. In the IPSD context, the policy cycle has five steps as the focus there is on the making and not the assessment of a policy per se, and as such policy analysis is regarded as a continuum throughout the whole policy process.

Conceptual Framework

IP focuses on three levels of integration:

1. The first is to consider significant ESE implications and interactions (vis-à-vis related criteria and indicators) associated with a policy problem and its potential solutions. The focus is on enhancing complementarities and reducing trade-offs among the ESE dimensions. The ESE inter-relations are stylized in Figure 2.1. Readers should note that although the ESE components are portrayed as equal spheres with inter-linkages for ease of presentation, the functioning of both economy and society ultimately depends on the environment.

Figure 2.1: Integrating ESE Dimensions of SD

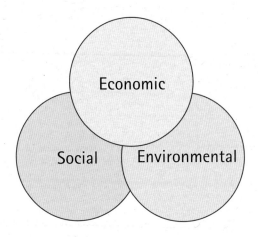

Figure 2.2: Policy Cycle

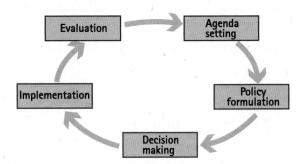

2. The second is to factor ESE considerations into the continuous policy cycle, especially at early stages. Policymaking, whether segmented or integrated, can be disaggregated into stages and sub-stages, which make up a "policy cycle" (see Figure 2.2) with the understanding that policymaking in practice is not linear or even sequential and is typically made up of multiple policy cycles without a clear starting point.

This reference manual uses a simple model, which begins with the consideration of a problem or issue that may arise from a previous policy (or the lack of a policy) and that requires government attention (agenda setting).[*] It then moves to the consideration of options to address the problem (policy formulation). In the third stage decision-makers prescribe a particular course of action (decision-making). In the fourth stage the prescribed course of action is translated into action (policy implementation). The results of the policy are then monitored and evaluated against its original aims, and adjustments to the policy, if needed, are made accordingly (policy evaluation, which includes monitoring). An "integration filter" is applied at every stage of the continuous policy cycle.

3. The third level of integration is to address policy constraints in terms of political support, administrative capacity, and analytical capacity within the policy process:

---

[*] A problem or an issue does not have to have negative connotations; an opportunity that is likely to miss without policy intervention can also be considered as a problem or an issue.

Political support is critical as integrated policies may represent major changes from the status quo, altering the existing balance of power and interests. Therefore, proactive political management with carefully crafted strategies is essential to generate and sustain the political support needed for such policies.

Administrative capacity refers to a government's capacity to formulate and carry out policies. Although this capacity is mostly associated with the implementation stage of a policy cycle, it is also relevant to the other stages such as the capacity to organize stakeholder consultations during agenda-setting.

Figure 2.5: Integrating Policy Objectives, Policy Environment, and Policy Process

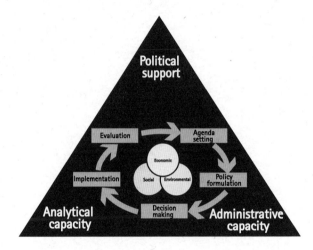

Analytical Capacity is critical for IP because multi-dimensional integrated policies tend to face more complexities and uncertainties than single-dimensional policies. Lack of such capacity may create a bias towards policies for which the effects can be analysed with greater certainty.

These components form a stylized strategic triangle in a policy environment, each playing an indispensable role in determining the extent of IP's success or failure. This strategic triangle (see Figure 2.5) needs to be considered in different stages of IP to determine: 1) constraints on IP; 2) areas where capacity building is needed; and 3) strategies complementing a particular policy in order to overcome deficiencies in the policy environment.

Agenda setting

In the context of public policy, an agenda is a list of issues or problems (including potential opportunities, which may be missed without policy interventions) to which government officials, and people outside of the government closely associated with those officials, are paying some serious attention at any given time. The agenda for a country might include, for example, rising food price, air pollution, and illegal immigration.

Of all the conceivable issues to which officials could be paying attention, they do seriously attend only to some rather than others. Thus, agenda-setting is a process in which policy initiators recognize that certain issues are public and are thus worthy of the government's attention, but the list of all possible issues for government action is narrowed to the set that actually becomes the focus of attention.

To factor ESE considerations into this initial stage of the policy cycle, four suggestions are highlighted:

- Frame the issue in sustainability terms;
- Harmonize the interests of different stakeholders;
- Manage the entry of an issue onto the agenda; and
- Seek policy windows.

Policy Formulation

Policy formulation is a process of generating policy options in response to a problem established on the agenda. This stage does not come automatically after an issue has gone onto the agenda. Nor is this stage the same as the decision-making stage where a course of action is to be chosen from the available options.[*] In this process, policy formulators – both inside and outside of the government – identify, refine, and formalize policy options to prepare the ground for the decision-making stage.

At this stage, some policy initiators may also take on the tasks of assessing and comparing the ESE implications and interactions of the potential options. However, such assessment and comparison typically requires investing a large amount of resources.

---

[*] The term "decision-making" used in this manual has a literal meaning as compared to the general use of the term, which tends to be equated with "policymaking".

Therefore it is generally agreed that such activities should take place after policy initiators have had a chance to conduct an initial screening of the potential options assessing their political, financial and administrative feasibility.

To factor SD considerations into this stage of the policy cycle, four suggestions are highlighted:

- Set up participatory, inter-agency mechanisms;
- Conduct root-cause analysis;

- Set policy objectives; and
- Formulate policy options.

Decision-making

Decision-making is not synonymous with policymaking. In public policy sciences, decision-making is described as a stage where a government decision-maker or an official decision-making body selects a course of action or non-action among a small set of policy options identified at the policy formulation stage with a view towards policy implementation.

Decision-making is highly political as the chosen course of action has the potential to create winners and losers, even in the case where it was decided to take no action, thus retaining the status quo. It can also be highly technical due to the complexity of the factors involved in assessing and comparing policy options based on their projected ESE consequences, which is supposed to be the basis for any integrated decision-making.

To advance the SD considerations, which have been carried through agenda-setting and policy formulation stages, into the decision-making stage, four suggestions are highlighted:

- Choose criteria for decision-making;
- Establish a baseline;
- Assess and compare policy options; and
- Make an informed decision.

Implementation

Implementation is the stage where a selected policy option must be translated into action. It is probably the most difficult, demanding, and critical stage in a policy process. Any deficiency in policy design or any vulnerability with respect to the policy environment will become visible at this stage. Yet implementation is often neglected in practice. Policy managers, initiators, formulators, decision-makers, and others involved in the policy process often fail to systematically prepare the ground for implementation, resulting in policies that perform far below expectation or even policy disasters.

The high degree of diversity among stakeholders involved in IP increases the complexity and vulnerability of implementation. Implementation creates winners and losers. It is the stage where the stakes of winning or losing begin to manifest themselves clearly to participants who have been left out of the earlier stages in the process. Most organizations may resist coordination due to a perceived threat to autonomy or disagreements over the nature of the tasks being pursued. Agencies and even divisions within agencies may compete for resources and control. Clashes may also occur among the public, private, non-profit, and community sectors.

To ensure that policies that have been subject to the rigorous SD "filtering" so far can receive a real chance to be implemented, i.e. achieve integration on the ground, four suggestions are highlighted:

- Consider implementation challenges throughout the policy cycle;
- Get organized and operational fast;
- Mobilize resources proactively; and
- Manage stakeholder dynamics.

Evaluation

Integrated evaluation refers to the effort to monitor and determine how a policy has fared during implementation from an SD perspective. It examines the means employed, the objectives served, and the effects caused in practice. The results and recommendations from evaluation are fed back into further rounds of policymaking. In many cases, some aspects of evaluation such as data collection are also conducted during earlier stages of policymaking and the results can feed into the refinement of policy design, decision and implementation.

Evaluation is expected to contribute to IP by:

- synthesizing what is known about a problem, its

proposed remedy, and the ESE effects from implementing that remedy, in order to facilitate policy learning;

- demystifying conventional wisdom or popular myths related to a problem, its solutions, and the effects of the solutions;

- developing new information about policy effectiveness, such as the extent to which expected policy results have been achieved and the range and magnitude of unintended effects, in order to give early warning; and

- explaining to all policy participants the implications of new information derived through evaluation, which may call for re-planning at the operational level.

To determine the actual effects of an implemented policy, not only on the objectives established for that policy, but also on the ESE dimensions of SD, four suggestions are highlighted:

- Specify the type, scope, and criteria of evaluation;
- Collect data and isolate policy effects;
- Conduct Participatory Monitoring and Evaluation (PME); and
- Ensure policy learning.

Conclusion

To gear public policies towards SD requires a genuine conviction of the need for SD on the part of governments and citizens. This, in turn, needs to come from a true appreciation of the risks from pursing particular societal objectives at the expense of other objectives and the opportunities from seeking synergies that exist among a society's ESE imperatives. Analysts can demonstrate these risks and opportunities through case studies. Advocacy groups and media can play an important role in communicating these risks and opportunities.

But even when individuals in the government and society are convinced of the need for SD and willing to apply IP, they face tremendous institutional and capacity constraints. To enhance such capacities and ease the transition towards IP, four suggestions are proposed and summarized below:

1. Demonstrate the risks of unsustainable

development and the opportunities from seeking synergies among ESE dimensions of SD in order to create genuine appreciation of the need for an integrated approach to policymaking;

2. Organize or reinvigorate an SD "policy community" to review national policy frameworks and institutional arrangements and propose improvements focusing on SD criteria and indicators as well as the effectiveness of related institutions;

3. Invest in sustainability-related statistical capacities in developing countries focusing on having an adequate number of qualified statisticians, acquiring and maintaining related data systems, and sustaining the regular data collection and reporting operations; and

4. Provide long-term as well as short-term training to create a critical mass of qualified policy analysts who can potentially assume the roles of policy managers, initiators, formulators, decision-makers, implementers, monitoring agents, and evaluators in support of IP.

1. Introduction

1.1 Definition

This manual provides guidance on IP with a view to promoting sustainable development (SD) in its environmental, social, and economic (ESE) dimensions. IP is proposed as a generic, normative public policymaking approach that considers significant ESE implications and interactions associated with public policy issues and their potential solutions. It also places solutions within a policy cycle that typically includes agenda-setting, policy formulation, decision-making, implementation, and evaluation, in order ensure that policy issues are appropriately defined, potential solutions compared, the solution that increases synergies and reduces trade-offs adopted, and the adopted solution implemented, monitored, and evaluated. Moreover, IP aligns policy development with the political, institutional, and analytical realities of the policy environment.

1.2 Audience

This manual has two levels of audience. The first is senior policy and decision makers in the public sector who wish to know IP's added value relative to their current policymaking approaches. The manual's executive summary and promotional materials will focus on this level of audience. The second, more pertinent audience for the purpose of this manual consists of the broadly defined policy practitioners who are already convinced of the merit of SD and seeking guidance on how to make public policies contribute to it. This level of audience includes not only policy managers, coordinators, and contact persons who sit in government offices, but also policy initiators, formulators, implementers, monitoring agents, evaluators, researchers, analysts, and other policy participants, often with overlapping functions, from both public and non-public institutions including at the international level. Additionally, members of academia are encouraged to utilize this manual.

1.3 Rationale

The need for an integrated approach to policymaking has been expressed in major international processes. The Millennium Development Goals (MDGs), for example, called for the "integration of the principles of sustainable development into country policies and programmes".[1] The World Summit on Sustainable Development (WSSD) emphasized the importance of taking a "holistic and inter-sector approach" to implement sustainable development.[2] The Millennium Ecosystem Assessment (MA) recommended the "integration of ecosystem management goals within other sectors and within broader development planning frameworks".[3]

In addition, a number of Multilateral Environmental Agreements (MEAs) have included clauses that require policy integration. Article Six of the Convention on Biological Diversity (CBD), for example, requires Parties to the Convention to "integrate, as far as possible and as appropriate, the conservation and sustainable use of biological diversity into relevant sectoral or cross-sectoral plans, programmes and policies".[4] Article Three of the United Nations Framework Convention on Climate Change (UNFCCC) also stipulates that "policies and measures to protect the climate system against human-induced change should... be integrated with national development programmes..."[5]

Introduction – Key points

- Consider Integrated Policymaking (IP) as a response to the call for proactive integration of sustainability considerations into public policymaking.
- Identify your particular entry point in a continuous policy cycle and go directly to the relevant parts of the manual for guidance.
- Adapt the materials in this manual and consult other related manuals to suit your circumstances, including time and financial constraints.

Box 1.1: Organizations working on Policy Integration

Many international organizations have implemented various initiatives, such as Strategic Environment Assessment (SEA), to promote policy integration. The Organization of Economic Co-operation and Development's Development Assistance Committee (OECD DAC), for example, provided guidance for applying SEA in the context of development co-operation in 2006.[6]

The United Nations Economic Commission for Europe (UNECE) launched an SEA protocol in 2003.[7] The European Commission (EC) initiated Sustainability Impact Assessment (SIA) of trade liberalization in 1999 and published a reference manual on trade-related SIA in 2006. In addition, in 2002 the EC required impact assessment of all major policy proposals in their ESE dimensions and in 2004, the EC SEA Directive took effect.[8]

Since 1997, the United Nations Environment Programme (UNEP) has been responding to the requests from over 30 developing countries and countries with economies in transition to conduct Integrated Assessment (IA) of public policies with a particular focus on trade-related policies and the agriculture sector.[9]

A number of institutions have responded to these calls for policy integration by promoting various sustainability-oriented assessments of public policies, programmes, and plans (see Box 1.1). UNEP has also worked for more than a decade in the field of integrated assessment, which has led to the launching of the IP initiative (see Box 1.2) and the publication of a dedicated IA manual, the *Integrated Assessment: Mainstreaming Sustainability into Policymaking*. The IP proposed in this manual builds on these assessment efforts and reinforces the response to the need for a proactive approach to integrating SD into policymaking. IP locks SD considerations into a policy process from the very beginning, before a policy issue is even brought onto the government agenda and certainly before any policy proposal is put on the table. In addition, IP

internalizes sustainability-oriented assessment without identifying it separately so as to make such assessment a natural and integral component of the policy process. This approach is expected to reduce the need for lagged, reactive analysis and improve the efficiency for decision-making in terms of cost and time as SD concerns are anticipated and addressed early on within the policy process.

IP – in its most intuitive sense of considering diverse factors when making policies – is important for at least three reasons. First, a policy that addresses one particular issue can affect other issues, which may not be less important. For example, perverse biofuel subsidies to reduce reliance on fossil fuels can contribute to food shortage and deforestation. Second, synergies among different issues exist and a policy intervention can be designed to achieve multiple benefits. Investing in basic health care, for example, not only contributes to poverty reduction, but also raises labour productivity. Third, successful implementation of a policy typically relies on the support from a range of stakeholders who may have diverse values and interests that need to be harmonized. For example, imposing anti-dumping duties on cheap imports may help protect domestic producers but may also hurt importers, retailers, and consumers at home.

1.4 User guidance

This document does not propose specific policies to address critical SD issues such as poverty, diseases, climate change, and conflicts. Rather, it provides generic guidance that can be applied to developing these and other policies in a way that contributes to SD. The readers should not expect to get specific policy prescriptions from this manual. Instead, they may want to utilize the stages and techniques described in this document in their respective policy situations to advance the course of SD.

This reference manual, complemented by the *Integrated Assessment: Guidance for Mainstreaming Sustainability into Policymaking*, is expected to promote an integrated approach to policymaking. Its follow-up activities are expected to include using the manual in support of various policy initiatives worldwide. UNEP, for example, will use the manual for the Green Economy Initiative, which encourages governments to invest in environmental sectors and

Box 1.2: The Development of the IP Manual

The work on IP embodied in this manual builds on four rounds of UNEP-sponsored IA country projects since 1997. In particular, it benefited from the results of the Integrated Assessment and Planning (IAP) projects completed in 2007.[10] In September 2005 when the preliminary results from the IAP projects started flowing in from nine participating countries, UNEP organized a consultative meeting to propose the development of a voluntary international framework for IA with an emphasis on integrated planning and policymaking. The proposal's objective was to produce a set of voluntary principles as well as reference materials to assist countries to implement such assessments. The overall goal was to ensure the integration of ESE considerations in planning and policymaking. The meeting welcomed such an initiative. Country representatives confirmed their need for a framework that would provide clear guidance for integrating SD into policies, highlighted key challenges in developing the framework, and emphasized the importance to implement such a framework in a flexible manner.

In February 2006, UNEP convened the second consultative meeting. The purpose was to discuss the preparation of the framework document. The meeting agreed that: a) the document should be prepared for policymakers as well as practitioners and it should reach beyond the environmental community; b) it should be user-friendly; c) it should emphasize policy integration and what has worked and what has not based on practical experiences in different countries; d) case studies should be used to demonstrate how integrated assessment can add value to decisions; and e) UNEP should take the initiative forward in partnership with a range of stakeholders. After this meeting, an effort was made to develop an outline of the document.

In the ensuing months, more complete results from the IAP projects became available, providing additional insights to the preparation of the framework document. It was found that the IAP process showed signs of success in a number of areas such as engaging stakeholders and identifying win-win opportunities, but as far as influencing the participating countries' internal policymaking is concerned, there was large room for improvement. In most cases, due to local political and institutional factors, the IAP exercises remained external to the official policy processes.

Reflecting on the IAP experience, building on the conclusions from the two consultative meetings, and in response to countries' needs, UNEP decided to focus the document on three areas where improvements could be made. First and foremost, there is a need to tap into the science (or art) of public policy in order to understand how policies are typically made in practice. On the basis of this understanding, it would be better able to identify a wider range of opportunities to factor SD considerations into the entire policy process rather than its particular stages. Second, there is a need to be more astute in managing stakeholder participation, especially in dealing with conflicts among different groups. Third, there is a need to improve the quality of policy analysis.

Based on these considerations, UNEP decided to switch from developing an IA framework document to preparing a reference manual in order to provide guidance on IP. A research team from the Lee Kuan Yew School of Public Policy at the National University of Singapore started developing the manual in September 2006. The team prepared the first draft in May 2007 when UNEP organized a review meeting involving representatives from governments, inter-governmental organizations, and non-governmental sector. Benefiting from the extensive comments from various partners, the team and UNEP staff revized the manual in July 2007. Subsequently, UNEP and its partners made substantive revisions until its publication.

green job creation in their responses to the financial and economic crisis. Additionally, UNEP will seek to work with economic development institutions to introduce the manual, promote its use on a voluntary basis, and get feedback at the country level. Given the diversity in country and policy circumstances, however, this manual does not envisage any institutionalization of IP at this time.

The rest of the manual is organized as follows. Chapter 2 presents the IP conceptual framework. Chapters 3 through 7 provide advice on how to manage the five core stages in the continuous policy cycle as they relate to IP. At the end of each Chapter from 3 to 7, there is an example using climate change as a broad illustration for the theme of the respective chapters. Chapter 8 concludes the manual.

It should be noted that policymaking is not typically a linear process. Different policy participants may also enter into a policy process at its different stages deploying appropriate "building blocks" of analytical and process-related tools. They may choose to use the index in the back of this manual and go directly to those parts of the manual that are of interest to their particular policy situations and entry points. To ensure an effective "plug-in", however, it is advisable to situate a particular entry point within the overall policy cycle presented in Figure 2.2 of Chapter 2. It is also advisable to link the types of processes and analyses suggested in this manual to the related legal requirements of each country, such as the SEA, in order to avoid repetitive processes. Moreover, users are encouraged to adapt the materials in this manual, take into account other related manuals, and develop guidance that is more relevant to their circumstances, priorities, and constraints.

References

1. United Nations, Millennium Development Goals (MDG), MDG7, Target 9.

2 "A journey of hope", Statement by the Chairman of the Preparatory Committee for WSSD, Mr. Emil Salim on the Final Day of the Second Session of the Committee, New York, 8 February 2002.

3. Millennium Ecosystem Assessment, 2005. *Ecosystems and Human Well-being*: *Synthesis*. Island Press, Washington, DC. P.20.

4. The Convention on Biological Diversity (CBD) 2006. *Article 6. General Measures for Conservation and Sustainable Development.* Retrieved March 2009 from www.cbd.int/convention/articles.

5. The United Nations Framework Convention on Climate Change (UNFCCC) 1994. *The Full Text of the Convention.* Retrieved March 2009 from http://unfccc.int/essential_background/ convention/background/items/1349.php

6. OECD, Applying Strategic Environmental Assessment – Good Practice Guidelines for Development Co-operation, DAC Guidelines and Reference Series, Paris, 2006.

7. United Nations Economic Commission for Europe (UNECE). (2003). *Protocol on Strategic Environmental Assessment.* Retrieved March 2009 from www.unece. org/env/eia/sea_protocol.htm

8. European Commission 2009 . *Impact Assessment: Political Context.* Retrieved March 2009 from ec.europa.eu/governance/impact/ index_en.htm

9. UNEP, Sustainable Trade and Poverty Reduction – New Approaches to Integrated Policy Making at the National Level, 2006.

10. UNEP IAP synthesis report.

2. Conceptual framework

This chapter presents the IP conceptual framework, which consists of integration at three levels. First, IP advocates the consideration of significant ESE implications and interactions associated with a policy problem and its potential solutions. Second, it seeks to factor ESE considerations into the continuous policy cycle. Third, it addresses constraints in terms of political support, administrative capacity, and analytical capacity within the policy process.

At the first level of integration, the relationships among the ESE dimensions of SD are often considered in trade-off terms, whereas their synergies are under-exploited. Reforming perverse energy subsidies, for example, is usually seen as undermining competitiveness, but the potential for encouraging investments in efficient technologies, thus enhancing competitiveness, is not considered. IP emphasizes the complementarities among the ESE dimensions of SD and seeks to reduce trade-offs.

At the second level, SD considerations, if attempted, are typically factored into policy formulation and decision-making stages when a particular course of action is about to be, or has been, chosen. The opportunities to frame a policy issue in SD terms and screen policy options against SD criteria at earlier stages of policymaking are thus under-exploited. IP

advocates a process in which ESE considerations are injected into the entire, ongoing policy process. This is not to treat policymaking as a linear process, but to seek every possible opportunity available in the policy cycle to integrate ESE considerations.

At the third level, even when a sound decision is made in SD terms, its implementation and evaluation can be problematic. The political, administrative, and analytical constrains on implementation and evaluation are often not considered explicitly and systematically when formulating policy recommendations. IP helps identify these constraints and proposes ways to enhance the necessary capacity as part of the policy process.

2.1 Integrating ESE dimensions

Most people continue using the Brundtland Commission's definition of SD – development that "meets the needs of the present without compromizing the ability of future generations to meet their own needs."[11] This concept's essence is to place socioeconomic development within the constraint of the environment. It is in this light that most people now consider SD and policies conducive to such development to include three dimensions: a) environmental integrity; b) social equity and justice; and c) economic prosperity. But these three dimensions

---

Conceptual framework – Key points

■ In the context of this manual, interpret the concept of "SD" or "Sustainability" in terms of significant ESE implications and interactions associated with a policy issue and its solution

■ Consider significant ESE implications and interactions in an integrated, comprehensive manner, bearing in mind that economies and societies fundamentally depend on the environment.

■ Consider significant ESE dimensions over a long time horizon when developing a policy and collect and report related data and information on a regular basis

■ Consider IP as a participatory and iterative process and apply an ESE "integration filter" at each stage of the continuous policy cycle in a practical, non-dogmatic manner.

■ Generate and sustain political support for integrated polices, ensure analytical and administrative capacity for IP, and devise strategies to overcome constraints in these areas.

are not of equal importance; fundamentally, economies and societies depend on the environment. If socioeconomic policies fail to take the environment into account, there will be consequences feeding back into socioeconomic systems.

Rather than trying to repeat what is known about the concept of SD and the relationships among its ESE dimensions, or come up with yet another way of interpreting these, for the purpose of this manual we observe that: a) many policy issues have ESE implications; b) policy solutions also have ESE implications and they should be checked against ESE criteria; c) ESE factors interact with each other to produce combined impacts. The ESE inter-relations are stylized in Figure 2.1. Readers should note that although the ESE components are portrayed as equal spheres with inter-linkages for ease of presentation, the functioning of both economy and society ultimately depends on the environment.

IP seeks to integrate the consideration of ESE factors to achieve the following objectives:

- Ensure policy decisions are acceptable with regard to each of the three dimensions;

- Identify innovative policies that will draw on the synergies among the three dimensions;

- Identify any trade-offs and propose remedial measures; and

- Increase the transparency and accountability of different stakeholders' attitudes towards different dimensions of SD.

Figure 2.1: Integrating ESE Dimensions of SD

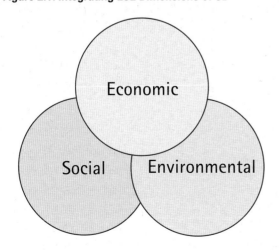

In practice, however the integration of the three dimensions may be stymied by several hurdles.

First, it is confronted by the prevailing, segmented policymaking found in many countries. Agencies responsible for specific sectors such as agriculture and forestry typically operate in isolation and uncoordinated with each other. The agricultural sector, for example, may pursue land conversion to expand farm production, which may contradict the forestry sector's policy to conserve wildlife habitats.

Second, environmental consequences often take a long time to materialize while policymakers typically have short-term horizons. It is, therefore, likely that long-term environmental dimensions of policy problems and deliberations are ignored while short-term socioeconomic outcomes are highlighted.

Third, tools for projecting socioeconomic changes as a result of a policy intervention are well established and relevant information is routinely collected, but the same cannot be said for environmental consequences. As a result, environmental consequences and implications, unlike their socioeconomic counterparts, are often poorly understood, poorly documented and, hence, likely to be ignored.

IP proposes several strategies to address these challenges. First, it encourages joint consideration of significant ESE dimensions associated with a policy issue. Second, it advocates the application of a long-term horizon to allow adequate consideration of significant ESE implications. Finally, IP requires continuous gathering and reporting of information on all three ESE dimensions. This manual will show to a certain extent how these strategies can be translated into actions in different stages of the policy process.

2.2 Integrating ESE criteria into policymaking

IP focuses on the entire, continuous policy process. This emphasis is based on two premises: 1) the opportunities for sustainability-oriented interventions may be found at every stage in policymaking; and 2) coordination among different policymaking stages is key to ensuring that an integrated approach is followed through.

Policymaking, whether segmented or integrated, can be disaggregated into stages and sub-stages, which make up a "policy cycle" (see Figure 2.2)[12]. There are various presentations of a policy cycle, but they are quite similar in essence, all reflecting how policies are made empirically. Thus the policy cycle presented in this manual is not a prescribed process or procedure of how things should happen, but a general sequence of how policies are made in practice.

For this manual, a simple model has been chosen, which begins with the consideration of a problem or issue that may arise from a previous policy (or the lack of a policy) that requires government attention (agenda setting).* It then moves to the consideration of options to address the problem (policy formulation). In the third stage, decision-makers prescribe a particular course of action (decision-making). In the fourth stage the prescribed course of action is translated into action (policy implementation). The results of the policy are then monitored and evaluated against the original aims and adjustments to the policy, if needed, are made accordingly (policy evaluation, which includes monitoring).

Figure 2.2 Policy Cycle

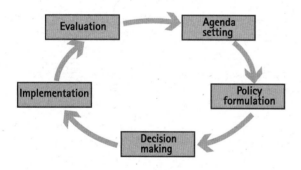

Policymaking in practice is not linear or even sequential and is typically made up of multiple policy cycles without a clear starting point. In many countries, policymaking may also be fragmented with lags in-between stages. Moreover, each stage has feedback loops with other stages reflecting the

dynamics of policymaking but such feedback loops are typically ignored in policymaking. All these elements need to be taken into account when applying IP, which should be considered as a problem-solving process with a lot of iterative refinement to manage public problems. In addition, it should be emphasized that this manual does not focus on the policy cycle per se, which is well established in public policy sciences, but on how to bring SD considerations into the different stages of the cycle.

In IP, an "integration filter" is applied at every stage of the continuous policy cycle. This broadens the venue for shaping policies in an integrated fashion. This approach, in particular, addresses the gaps between sustainability-oriented decision-making and implementation, as critical deficiencies in implementing capacity are identified at the outset. In addition, by focusing on the entire, continuous policy cycle, IP addresses the policy breach between decision-making and evaluation. Finally, through its emphasis on participatory policymaking and inter-ministerial coordination, IP not only connects the various stages of the policy process within a particular sector, but also brings together policy processes across sectors, thereby making integration a shared objective among sectoral policymakers. Figure 2.3 illustrates the overlay of the ESE dimensions onto a policy cycle.

Superimposing the ESE considerations over the making of a particular policy, however, faces a number of challenges, which are highlighted in Table 2.1. Later chapters will provide guidance on how to address these challenges.

Figure 2.3 An Integration Filter for a Policy Cycle

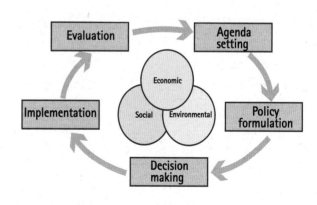

---

* A problem or an issue does not have to have negative connotations; an opportunity that is likely to miss without policy intervention can also be considered as a problem or an issue.

Table 2.1: Challenges to Integrating ESE Dimensions into a Policy Cycle

Stage in Policy Cycle	IP's Roles	Main Challenges
Agenda-Setting	To bring problems of public concern onto agenda by defining the problems in relation to SD priorities, risks, and opportunities	• SD considerations are typically long-term, difficult to compete with short-term issues for policymakers' attention. • Defining policy issues in SD terms may affect vested interests, which can block the entry of these issues onto agenda. • Even if SD considerations are factored into problem definition, they may be subject to deliberate misinterpretation.
Policy Formulation	To develop feasible options that will address the ESE root causes of the problems	• Applying an ESE filter to policy formulation requires additional cost and cross-sectoral analytical capacity, which may not be readily available. • Expanding the scope of potential solutions requires the participation of a larger number of stakeholders, which can be costly and time-consuming. • Budget constraint limits the number of options to consider
Decision-Making	To adopt options that meet SD criteria and are acceptable to stakeholders	• Data gaps, weak analytical capacity, and uncertainty (often associated with SD) tend to weaken the basis for sound decision-making. • Decisions are often the results of compromises (including compromises among ESE interests), although these may not be always satisfactory to all stakeholders. • Decisions may be rushed due to external forces or sudden events that require immediate responses, such as in a post-conflict or post-disaster situation.
Implementation	To adopt options that meet SD criteria and are acceptable to stakeholders	• The decisions made are not always followed up with designated implementation agencies and earmarked budget, making the decisions stay on paper. • The required level of implementation may exceed the capacity and budget of the implementing agency. • Implementation may proceed initially within the capacity and budget of the implementing agency, but it may soon wear out the capacity and depletes the budget without replenishment. • Unexpected problems may pop up affecting implementation (e.g. failure in inter-agency cooperation), but there is often no mechanism to redress them and allow implementation to continue.
Evaluation	To review implementation of the adopted policies against pre-selected objectives as well as criteria reflecting SD considerations	• Sustainability impacts often take long time to be felt. • The effects of a particular policy are often interwoven with other policies and events, making it difficult to isolate the impacts. • There may be resistance to substantive evaluation as the result could be unfavourable to those who design, decide, and implement the policy.

2.3 Integrating Policy Environment into Policymaking

To address the challenges outlined in Table 2.1, policy managers need to pay attention to three factors that typically constitute a policy environment: political support, administrative capacity, and analytical capacity.

Political support is critical because policymakers must continually attract both legitimacy and resources from their authorizing institutions and constituencies. Integrated policies may represent major changes from the status quo. Conflicts both inside and outside the government over the nature of these changes can be expected, as different stakeholders have different viewpoints, needs, interests, information, and sources of power. Proactive political management with carefully crafted strategies are, therefore, essential for generating and sustaining the political support needed for such policies.

Administrative capacity refers to a government's capacity to formulate and carry out policies. Typical aspects of this capacity include the quality of civil service, the use of information technology, the inter-agency relations, and the style of interactions between the government and society. Although administrative capacity is mostly associated with the implementation stage of a policy cycle, it is also relevant to the other stages such as the capacity to organize stakeholder consultations at the agenda-setting stage.

Analytical Capacity is critical for IP because multi-dimensional integrated policies tend to face more complexities and uncertainties than single-dimensional policies. The information overload together with the lack of specific and useful information places further constraints on analytical capacity. Lack of such capacity may create a bias towards policies for which the effects can be analysed with greater certainty.

These components form a stylized strategic triangle in a policy environment, each playing an indispensable role in determining the extent of IP's success or failure (see Figure 2.4).

The strategic triangle presented in Figure 2.5 is to be considered in different stages of IP to serve the following purposes:

- To identify constraints on IP. Analytical capacity determines the potential usefulness of IP in improving the quality of policy decisions. Political support and administrative capacity constrain the types of polices that can be realistically made.
- To identify areas where capacity building is needed. Unlike traditional policy analysis in which capacity constraints are regarded as given, IP through considering the policy environment can include capacity-building activities as part of policymaking.
- To determine strategies required to complement a particular policy in order to overcome deficiencies in the policy environment. The consideration of timing and sequencing of policy actions, for example, can also be incorporated as part of such strategies.

References

11. The World Commission on Environment and Development (The Brundtland Commission), *Our Common Future*, p.43, Oxford University Press, Oxford, UK, 1987.

12. Howlett, M, and M. Ramesh. (2003) *Studying Public Policy: Policy Cycles and Policy Subsystems*, Oxford University Press.

Figure 2.4 Strategic Triangle of a Policy Environment

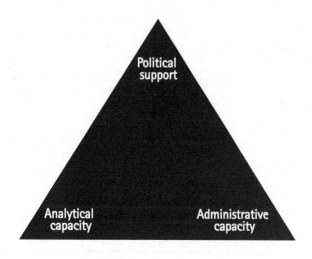

Figure 2.5 Integrating Policy Objectives, Policy Environment, and Policy Process

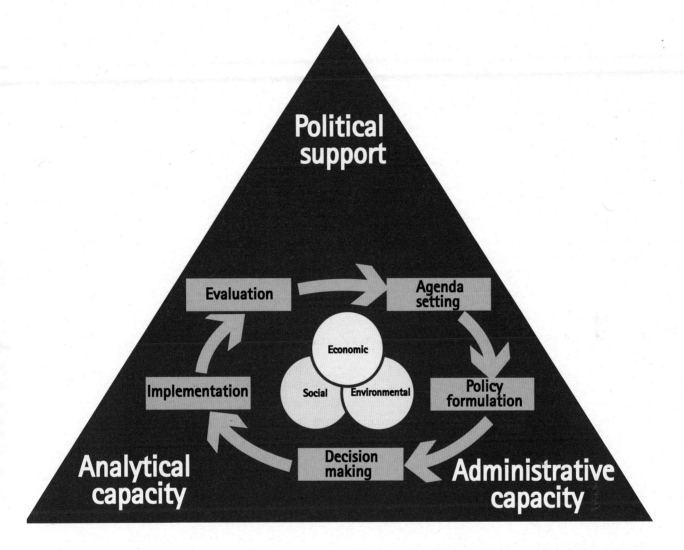

Agenda setting – Key points

Framing the issue in sustainability terms

■ Define your issue in relation to the society's SD context, including priorities, risks and opportunities.

■ Link your issue to other sectors' or groups' concerns as well as other related policy issues and processes that may affect your issue and the potential solutions to your issue.

■ Create multi-stakeholder forums to facilitate integrated and harmonized framing of your issue.

■ Keep the definition of your issue specific and guard against "hijacking" of the issue definition by particular interest groups.

■ Establish facts, evidences, and arguments for your issue and communicate them effectively to the public as well as government policy managers with a focus on the potential for win-win opportunities from addressing your issue.

Harmonizing the interests of different stakeholders

■ Avoid sectoral and institutional biases when participating in issue definition.

■ Facilitate convergence of views and issues among diverse stakeholders and use "relevance to SD" as a pre-requisite for the entry of an issue to the agenda.

■ Provide relevant information and help societal policy initiators navigate the route to government agenda.

■ Conduct, facilitate, and institutionalize public consultations for government-led initiatives.

Managing the entry of an issue onto the agenda

■ Control which issues to take on board based on their strategic and critical relevance to SD priorities, government's issue-preparedness, and stakeholder support – all requiring strategizing by policy managers.

■ Establish horizontal and vertical linkages within the government and with social actors to ensure successful entry of an issue to the agenda.

■ Engage analysts to conduct high-quality issue analysis, drawing on related, previous studies.

■ Support development of administrative and analytical capacity.

Seeking policy windows

■ Need to compete to get your issue onto the agenda.

■ Link your issue to the successive iterations of a previous policy cycle or major events and, where possible:

■ Utilize institutionalized policy windows such as regular planning and budgeting cycles

■ Be prepared well in advance for various policy windows with high-quality issue analysis and good government contacts

3. Agenda setting

In the context of public policy, an agenda is a list of issues or problems (including potential opportunities which may be missed without policy interventions) to which government officials, and people outside of the government closely associated with those officials, are paying some serious attention at any given time.[13] The agenda for a country might include, for example, rising food price, air pollution, illegal immigration, and energy security.

Of all the conceivable issues to which officials could be paying attention, they do seriously attend only to some rather than others. Thus, agenda-setting is a process in which policy initiators recognize that certain issues are public and are thus worthy of the government's attention, but the list of all possible issues for government action is narrowed to the set that actually becomes the focus of attention. [14]

This chapter provides guidance on how ESE considerations can be factored into this initial stage of the policy cycle. It covers four major aspects of integrated agenda-setting: 1) framing the issue in SD terms; 2) harmonizing the interests of different stakeholders; 3) managing the entry of an issue onto the agenda; and 4) seeking policy windows. These are not clear-cut, sequential steps in agenda-setting; anyone who is involved in policy development may have to handle these activities simultaneously. It should also be noted that major "building blocks" of analytical and process-related tools such as baseline analysis, trend analysis, communication, stakeholder participation, etc. permeate all these steps and are often relevant to other stages of the policy process. They are often described in other related manuals and are, therefore, not fully covered in this manual.[15] An illustrative example is provided at the end of the chapter.

3.1 Framing issues in SD terms

Integrated agenda-setting requires policy initiators to frame their issues in relation to a society's SD context, including related priorities, risks, and opportunities. This also implies the consideration of other sectors' and groups' concerns, as well as other related policy issues and processes that may affect the issues at hand and their potential solutions. If the problem of low enrolment rate for girls were defined merely as an education problem, for example, the issue might not receive adequate attention from the government and the parents. But if it were framed as an SD problem affecting the health of future generations, population pressure on natural resources, labour productivity, and economic growth, it may receive a rather different reaction.

Many environmental groups are already adopting this approach and start articulating environmental issues in connection with poverty reduction, economic growth, trade, and business profits, thereby expanding the constituency to address environmental issues. Similarly, when some consumer groups articulate the issue of food safety, they not only discuss health concerns, but also the implications of unsafe food for the competitiveness of food exports, thereby motivating stakeholders in the export sector to support moving the issue of food safety onto the agenda. Government policy managers can create multi-stakeholder commissions and task forces or other forms of inquiries to facilitate such integrated interpretations of the issues with a focus on proactively identifying inter-sectoral linkages and potential win-win opportunities for different stakeholders upfront. This will enable them to sequence and bundle related policy issues as well as their solutions.

Framing a policy problem in an integrated manner does not mean, however, that the problem should be defined in general and vague terms. To the contrary, policy initiators should define a problem as clearly and concretely as possible, covering its size or extent. For example, if excessive urban air pollution is a problem, the policy initiator should describe the extent of the problem by showing the types and volumes of the pollutants emitted, the number of people affected, the economic losses suffered, and the trends in the coming years. Established ESE standards and commitments, national or international, should be used as critical factors to illustrate the magnitude of the problem. In defining a problem, it is also important that policy initiators should not define the potential solution into the problem. For example, one may define the lack of parking space in a city as a problem, but this definition has a built in bias towards the solution of building more parking space. A proper definition may be: there are too many cars relative to the parking space available.[16]

In this regard, policy initiators should also be aware of the competing efforts to define an issue. Each may generate its own conclusions about the right solutions. Take climate change, as an example, some groups frame the problem of carbon emissions in aggregate terms, i.e. the total amount currently emitted by each country, whereas others frame the issue in per capita terms, each with different implications for potential solutions. Similarly, some groups define the issue of energy subsidy as perverse incentives that encourage excessive carbon emissions whereas other groups are more concerned that these subsidies do not reach the poor as the intended beneficiaries. Policy initiators and government policy managers need to conduct "contextual scans", harmonize different perspectives, but also ensure that one definition does not exclude others in a way that derails the effort to solve the issue.

This points to the importance of gathering facts, evidences, and arguments to substantiate the critical nature of the issue and, based on these "ammunitions", communicating the issue effectively. Doing such "homework" well will enhance the chance of getting the issue onto the agenda. Climate change, for example, is now established as a top international agenda, but this is inseparable from decades of fact-gathering efforts. The Al Gore movie of "An Inconvenient Truth" and the Stern report on the economics of climate change are influential vehicles to communicate the facts and help anchor the issue to the agenda.

3.2 Harmonizing the interests of different stakeholders

In essence, linking a policy issue to SD priorities and to the concerns of others requires harmonizing the interests of different stakeholders who represent different SD dimensions. Policy initiators from the industrial and business sectors, therefore, are advised to reach out to other groups when seeking

government actions on the issues of their concern. At the same time, policy initiators from NGOs and civil society groups need to exercise caution against one-sided or limited, short-term visions of policy problems and solutions.

An example is some groups' strong opposition to expanding the development of nuclear energy as a substitute for fossil fuels. These groups have until recently succeeded in preventing the issue from moving onto the official agenda in Europe, but other groups may consider such a position to be biased, ignoring the potential gains in reducing carbon emissions and the safety-related technological advances that have been achieved in this sector in recent years. This manual does not take a position on the issue per se; what it does argue for is openness to different perspectives and effort to resolve the differences through an iterative process.

This cooperation among different policy initiators is critical if an issue is to successfully proceed through to the governmental agenda and beyond. If this cooperation were not forthcoming, or the goals between the government and the societal groups were too diffuse, the government might have to neutralize or co-opt certain groups in order to move forward what it believes to be an important agenda. This, however, can slowdown the policymaking process and render its outcomes uncertain. It can, for example, allow certain groups to counter-mobilize and advocate alternative conceptions of policy problems and solutions, or demand the withdrawal of an item from the government agenda. Government policy managers are, therefore, advised to "get out in front" of an issue and facilitate the convergence of views among different social groups.

Integrated agenda-setting encourages the involvement of diverse stakeholders in raising and defining policy issues. In such a process, someone or some group can initiate an issue by articulating a grievance and demanding its resolution by the government. The same policy initiator can then attempt to expand support for its demand, a process that may involve submerging specific complaints within more general ones in a process of "issue aggregation" (this is where, for example, the linkage to a society's SD priorities can be established) and alliance-building across groups. Finally, the policy initiator can lobby, contest, and join with others in getting the issue onto the government agenda. The modern environmental movement, which has brought about numerous environmental laws and regulations all over the world, for example, is often traced to Rachel Carson's 1962 publication of "Silent Spring".[18]

None of the outside policy initiators' activities are, however, without difficulties and official agenda access is by no means guaranteed or automatic. To succeed, these initiators must have the requisite political resources and skills to outmanoeuvre their opponents or advocates of other issues and actions.

Sympathetic government policy managers can facilitate these initiators' articulation of issues and concerns, for example, by providing information on substantive issues or governmental processes, which can help outside policy initiators navigate the route to the government agenda.[19] These policy managers can also require outside policy initiators to frame their issues in relation to a society's SD priorities as a pre-requisite for entering onto the government agenda.

There are many cases where policy issues are raised within the government. In such cases, government policy managers need to ensure that senior officials

---

Box 3.1: Public consultation

Checklist

- Objective ("what you want to get out of it"): "finding new ideas (brainstorming); collecting factual data; validating a hypothesis; etc."
- What to consult on (different elements of a policy problem): "nature of the problem, objectives and policy options, impacts, comparison of policy options" or "whole draft proposal".
- Whom to consult: "general public, restricted to a specific category of stakeholders (any member in the selected category can participate) or limited to a set of designated individuals/organizations (only those listed by their name can participate)..."always include all target groups and sectors which will be significantly affected by or involved in policy implementation...".
- When to consult: "should start as early as possible in order to maximize its impacts on policy development", "should be seen as a recurring need in the policy development process rather than 'one-off' event", "useful to arrange a series of consultations as the proposal develops" along the various stages of the policy cycle.
- How to consult: "consultative committees, expert groups, open hearings, ad hoc meetings, consultation via internet, questionnaires, focus groups, seminar/workshops, etc."

Minimum standards

- Provide consultation documents that are clear, concise and include all necessary information.
- Consult all relevant target groups.
- Ensure sufficient publicity and choose tools adapted to the target group(s)...
- Leave sufficient time for participation...
- Publish the results of public consultation...
- Provide acknowledgement of responses...
- Provide feedback: report on the consultation process, its main results and how the opinions expressed have been taken into account...

Pitfalls

- Not to be unduly influenced by the views of one particular group, no matter how professionally these have been presented.
- Consultation can never be a substitute for analysis of an issue.
- Don't repeat consultations unless you are seeking additional opinions/information, or unless there is new information to present to them.

Source: The EC, IA Guidelines.

---

hold meetings and engage in public consultations. Such processes can range from public hearings and opinion polling requiring only a response to a survey to the attendance of representatives of political parties, interest groups, or other individuals in formal hearing venues such as presidential or parliamentary commissions. They could also grant greater autonomy to the media, ease public access to the relevant information, create space for civil society to operate and make their views known, authorize different government departments – not just the lead department – to comment on issues, and provide resources for research institutes and think tanks to conduct issue analysis.

Policy managers can also institutionalize stakeholder consultations. Advisory committees, commissions, task forces, and roundtables are all forms of government-appointed bodies for developing problem definitions that are acceptable to both social and state actors, who will then have a better chance to successfully negotiate the remaining stages of the policy process. The appointment of members of the public to these and other institutional bodies is a means of increasing the representation of non-organized public interests, both at the agenda-setting stage and throughout the entire policy process.

Consultation is a recurrent theme throughout a policy cycle. To ensure effectiveness and efficiency, policy managers should carefully plan consultations. The EC provided practical guidance in this regard, which is reproduced in Box 3.1.[20] This guidance is an example of "building blocks", which can be applied during different stages of the policy cycle.

3.3 Managing the entry of an issue onto the agenda

Policy managers promoting integrated agenda-setting should facilitate the entrance of strategic and critical issues that are highly relevant to a society's SD priorities and issues that they are prepared to deal with on the basis of a good understanding of the possible causes and solutions as well as the support of stakeholders. At the same time, they should consider hindering or delaying the entrance of those issues that are not highly relevant to established SD priorities, whose potential solutions and stakeholder support are unclear, and to which they can only respond in an unprepared and ad hoc manner.

To exert effective control described above, government policy managers need to monitor their societies and understand the ways in which various critical factors – conditions, actors, institutions, and interests – affect agenda-setting and the likely direction of the move of any issues from the public to official agendas. They need to:

- Understand the government's political orientation (e.g. pro-market or pro-government), administrative and analytical capacity, the preferences and capacity of the societal actors, and the inter-relationships among different actors;

- Be strategic in creating and interacting with "policy communities" – networks of government and societal stakeholders who are interested in a common issue and who conduct discourse on the issue on an ongoing basis;

- Ensure that the participation in policy communities is representative and open, yet not so heterogeneous as to make the emergence of shared understanding of a problem impossible;

- Establish lead coordinating agencies within the government to identify areas of convergence and divergence among the issues arising from agenda-setting.

In addition, policy managers also need to have the links to other parts and levels of the government and to relevant political and social actors. Futhermore, they need trained analysts capable of teasing out the implications of multiple problem definitions and the inter-relationships of problems and potential solutions, drawing on previous studies. This would help avoid perverse or sub-optimal outcomes due to partial or incomplete analysis. It would also help ensure that key actors are not mobilized to oppose policy solutions congruent with the integrated approach.

However, whether or not they will be able to conduct contextual scans, diagnose the issues, project trends, and develop strategies for such agenda management, depends to a large extent on their administrative and analytical capacities – the kind of information, personnel, and funding they have at their disposal to conduct issue analysis. Senior government officials and external agencies supporting integrated approach to policymaking can provide targeted support to enhance these capacities systematically.

3.4 Seeking policy windows

The prioritization implicit in agenda-setting means that policy initiators, in or outside of the government, have to compete with each other for their respective issues to be placed on the agenda. Policy managers in government agencies often have control over this competition. After the breakout of the Severe Acute Respiratory Syndrome (SARS) in Asia in 2004, for example, different groups sought to advance their respective issues onto the policy agenda: transparency and accountability of the government, intellectual property rights to viruses and vaccines, consumption of wildlife, the plight of rural farmers, and mechanisms of rapid response to outbreaks of diseases. Eventually, however, government policy managers only took some of these issues on board.

Policy initiators need to understand that if their issues out-compete other issues and get on to the agenda, early solutions will be generated. One technique to get your issue onto the agenda ahead of others is to closely link the issue to the successive iterations of a previous policy cycle. In re-negotiating the Economic Partnership Agreements with the EU, for example, the African, Caribbean, and Pacific (ACP) States have brought issues of their concern to the table, such as opening up their markets to the EU and phasing-out EU's preferential prices for the export of sugar from these countries. Another technique is to seize windows of opportunities amid major events, such as change of government, conflicts, economic recession, natural disasters, and major sports events such as the Olympic Games, to place their issues on the agenda. The unfortunate reality, however, is that these techniques are not reserved exclusively for use by sustainability-minded policy initiators; anyone can make use of these techniques to advance the issues of their concern. This reality once more underscores the importance to compete for policy attention.

In most cases, institutionalized opportunities such as periodic elections or budgetary cycles exist in which policy initiators can promote policies and policy processes. Most policy windows open quite predictably. Legislation comes up for renewal on schedule, for instance, creating opportunities to change, expand or abolish certain policies and programmes. This is true for routine, institutionalized planning exercises as well such as multi-year national development planning, the review of poverty reduction strategies in low income countries, and operational programming under the EC's Structural Funds. These processes are conducted to evaluate or assess on-going policy initiatives and consider new ones, typically covering a large number of socioeconomic sectors. Policy initiators need to make themselves aware of these recurrent cycles and their internal deadlines. They need to plan ahead to make full use of these opportunities so that their issues and concerns will be identified and addressed.

There may also be cases where individual senior officials have the power to bring issues onto the agenda at discretion. If policy managers and initiators had anticipated such windows and prepared relevant issue definition, analysis, and potential solutions, they could shape the solutions in a comprehensive manner. But such policy windows may not be common in practice. Rather than relying on discretionary windows, therefore, policy initiators are advised to focus on institutionalized windows or crisis windows.

Predictable or not, open windows are scarce and often temporary. Policy initiators must, therefore, have the capacity to identify the types of windows available for their issues to enter onto the government agenda and be prepared to promote solutions to problems when an opportunity arises. The agenda-setting strategy that a policy initiator devises, then, should consider the existence of different kinds of policy windows.

Understanding, identifying, and preparing for policy windows and even shaping such windows requires the recruitment, training, and retention of specialized policy analysts charged with carrying out these duties and the careful cultivation of contacts within and outside the government. Major environmental groups in the US, for example, all have staff members performing these functions in the name of "Congressional Relations". Journalists tracking specific lines of issues are also excellent in keeping an eye on potential policy windows.

Policy managers have a unique role to play in seeking policy windows. They should watch emerging critical issues so that they can take advantage of policy windows when they open. They should use their knowledge of the emerging problems to inform the society by releasing relevant information and running public campaigns if necessary. They could also provide privileged access to the groups that they can work with and that do have an integrated perspective.

Illustration: Establishing climate change on the international agenda

Climate change as a public policy issue is now established in policy agenda at the international level as well as in many countries. The issue was first brought up by scientists in 1972 at the United Nations Scientific Conference in Stockholm. It was framed in terms of pollutants of global significance. The Conference called for monitoring efforts to be coordinated by the World Meteorological Organization (WMO).

In 1979 the first "World Climate Conference" organized by the WMO expressed concern that "continued expansion of man's activities on earth may cause significant extended regional and even global changes of climate". It called for "global cooperation to explore the possible future course of global climate and to take this new understanding into account in planning for the future development of human society." The Conference appealed to nations of the world "to foresee and to prevent potential man-made changes in climate that might be adverse to the well-being of humanity". In 1985 a joint UNEP/WMO/ICSU Conference on the "Assessment of the Role of Carbon Dioxide and of Other Greenhouse Gases in Climate Variations and Associated Impacts" concluded, that "as a result of the increasing greenhouse gases it is now believed that in the first half of the next century (21st century) a rise of global mean temperature could occur which is greater than in any man's history."*

In 1987, as evidence of climate change was emerging, the UN General Assembly adopted the "Environmental Perspective to the Year 2000 and Beyond". This document introduced the concept of sustainable development for the first time and subsumed climate change under the issue of energy. It became increasingly recognized that policymakers need an objective source of information about the

* Extracts from the IPCC 10th Year Anniversary Brochure http://www.ipcc.ch/pdf/10th-anniversary/anniversary-brochure.pdf

causes of climate change, its potential environmental and socio-economic consequences and the adaptation and mitigation options to respond to it. To that end, WMO and UNEP established the Intergovernmental Panel on Climate Change (IPCC) in 1988 which provides the decision-makers and others interested in climate change with an objective source of information. 1989 may be considered a year when climate change was formally established on the international agenda. The General Assembly in resolution 44/207 "endorsed the UNEP Governing Council's request to begin preparations with WMO for negotiations on a framework convention on climate change".

The IPCC First Assessment Report in 1990 concluded that human activities were indeed responsible for climate change and served as the basis for the set up of a United Nations Intergovernmental Negotiating Committee for a Framework Convention on Climate Change (INC/FCCC) to coordinate the efforts between governments in addressing the problems associated with climate change. The INC organized 5 meetings between 1991 and 1992, which gathered more than 150 nations. The discussions included topics such as the need for an international commitment, the setting of measurable objectives and timeline for greenhouse gas reduction, the establishing of financial mechanisms, facilitating technology transfer, and defining different levels of responsibilities to meet the climate change challenge. In order to meet its objectives, the INC required a binding agreement between all involved parties.

The United Nations Framework Convention on Climate Change (UNFCCC) was therefore established in May 1992 and formally entered into force on 21 March 1994 with the backing of over 50 nations.

In 1995 at the first conference of the parties (COP) of the UNFCCC, held in Berlin, the parties (UNFCCC member countries) started negotiations on what was to become the Kyoto Protocol. The Berlin Mandate established a two-year analysis and assessment phase of action to reduce greenhouse gases. In 1997, the Kyoto Protocol was adopted after intense negotiations and became the first international agreement linked to the United Nations Framework Convention on Climate Change, which sets binding targets for industrialized countries for reducing greenhouse gas

(GHG) emissions. These amount to an average of five per cent against 1990 levels over the five-year period 2008-2012.

As of December 2008, the UNFCCC has held 14 conferences of the parties (COPs) which have helped bring climate change on the top of countries agenda. The 15th COP to be held in Copenhagen in December 2009 is expected to lead to a post-Kyoto protocol.

Further Reading

Kingdon, J. W. (1984). *Agendas, Alternatives, and Public Policies.* Boston, Little Brown and Company.

Rochefort, D. A. and R. W. Cobb (1994). *The Politics of Problem Definition: Shaping the Policy Agenda.* Lawrence, University of Kansas Press.

Baumgartner, F. R. and B. D. Jones (1991). "Agenda Dynamics and Policy Subsystems." *Journal of Politics* 53(4): 1044-1074.

Birkland, T. A. (1998). "Focusing Events, Mobilization, and Agenda Setting." *Journal of Public Policy* 18(1): 53-74.

Cobb, R. W., M. H. Ross, et al. (1997). *Cultural Strategies of Agenda Denial; Avoidance, Attack and Redefinition.* Lawrence, University Press of Kansas.

Hammond, T. H. (1986). "Agenda Control, Organizational Structure, and Bureaucratic Politics." *American Journal of Political Science* 30(2): 379-420.

Stone, D. A. (1989). "Causal Stories and the Formation of Policy Agendas." *Political Science Quarterly* 104(2): 281-300.

References

13. Kingdon, J. W. (1984). *Agendas, Alternatives, and Public Policies.* Boston, Little Brown and Company.

14. Spector, M. and J. I. Kitsuse (1987). *Constructing Social Problems.* New York, Aldine de Gruyter.

15. Maria do Rosario Patidario, Strategic Environmental Assessment Good Practices Guide Methodological Guidance, Portuguese Environment Agency, 2007.

16. E. Bardach, p7. EC IA Guidelines p17.

17. The Economist. (2006). *The Nuclear Power Debate.* Retrieved March 2009 from http://www.economist.com/displaystory.cfm?story_id=7959969

18. Carson, R. (1962). Silent Spring. Publisher Houghton Mifflin

19. Milward, H. B. and G. L. Walmsley (1984). Policy Subsystems, Networks and the Tools of Public Management. *Public Policy Formation.* R. Eyestone. Greenwich, JAI Press: 3-25.

20. The EC IA Guidelines, p10-12.

Policy formulation – Key points

Setting up participatory, inter-agency mechanisms

- Organize inter-agency committees or taskforces to formulate policy collectively or independently as appropriate, involve senior officials and opinion leaders as well as potential policy implementers, monitors, and evaluators.

- Adopt rules for resolving conflicts.

- Make use of inputs from independent policy communities, support the participation of non-state actors including marginal groups and women in such communities, encourage open exchanges, ensure the quality of public participation, and support anticipatory analysis and knowledge creation.

- Note that setting up these mechanisms is one of the "building blocks", which may take place in any stage of the policy cycle.

Conducting root-cause analysis

- Analyse the causes of the issue in question, including the baseline and trends of these causes and how events and policies may affect these causes overtime.

- Use a combination of analytical models to get a comprehensive picture, covering the market model (focusing on the role of market forces), production model (focusing on the role of the government), and evolutionary model (focusing on attitudinal factors).

- Choose analytical tools under each model based on the consideration of data requirements, cost of application, capability to deal with uncertainties, and the level of transparency in the analytical process.

- Note that causality analysis is a "building block", which may be used at any stage of the policy cycle such as the agenda-setting stage to analyse the implications, risks, threats, opportunities, cumulative effects, and feedback loops associated with an issue in question if left unaddressed, thus strengthen the case for the entrance of the issue into agenda.

Setting policy objectives

- Establish a limited number of objectives for the potential policy solution, targeting the problem of concern and its causes.

- Differentiate between different levels of the policy objectives as appropriate, typically at general, specific and operational levels.

- Make objectives SMART: Specific, Measurable, Accepted, Realistic, and Time-bound.

- Assess the consistency between contemplated objectives and the society's established SD objectives.

- Confirm and publicize agreed policy objectives for the potential policy solutions.

Formulate policy options

- Anticipate difficulties when proposing comprehensive policy options that seek fundamental changes from the *status quo.*

- Consider appropriate extent, sequence, and pace of changes implied by policy options.

- Borrow comparable experience from elsewhere in seeking effective policy solutions.

- Look for policy solutions from the government's toolbox.

- Bundle related policy issues and use a combination of policy solutions to achieve multiple effects.

- Mobilize the private sector in solving public policy issues.

- Weed out clearly unfeasible policy options on political, financial, or administrative grounds, but do not consider these constraints to be insurmountable – some constraints may be overcome.

4. Policy formulation

Policy formulation is a process of generating policy options in response to a problem established on the agenda. This stage does not come automatically after an issue has gone onto the agenda. Mainstreaming gender issues, for example, was established as a global agenda item at the 1995 United Nations Fourth World Conference on Women, but it has rarely been translated into action at the national level. Nor is this stage the same as the decision-making stage where a course of action among options is to be chosen.[21] In this process, policy formulators identify, refine and formalize policy options to prepare the ground for the decision-making stage.

At this stage, policy initiators may also take on the tasks of assessing and comparing the ESE implications and interactions of the potential options. However, such assessment and comparison typically requires investing a large amount of resources. Therefore it is generally agreed that such activities should take place after policy initiators have had a chance to conduct an initial screening of the potential options assessing their political, financial and administrative feasibility. Since such assessment and comparisons are sequentially closer to the moment of decision-making and for presentational reasons (to balance the length of different chapters), these activities are covered in Chapter 5: Decision-making.

Policy formulators can come from both inside and outside of the government.[22] Within the government, career bureaucrats draft policy documents, senior officials lead government agencies and direct commissions and task forces, and legislators develop new legislation and conduct legislative reviews. Outside of the government, the non-official sector including businesses, professional associations, civil society groups, and media assess proposed policy options – typically prompted by perceived impacts that may arise from initially proposed policies – and feed them into the governmental process. International organizations also offer policy options on issues of global dimension such as climate change, epidemics, conflicts, and financial crisis, but they are encouraged to rely on, or at least involve local experts in formulating policy options.

This chapter describes how SD considerations can be factored into this stage in the policy cycle. It focuses on four steps of integrated policy formulation: a) establishing participatory, inter-agency mechanisms to be responsible for developing policy options; b) conducting an ESE-integrated causal analysis of the established issue; c) setting the objectives for potential policy solutions; d) prioritizing a limited number of policy options. Although these steps appear to have some sequential logic, they are not to be followed rigidly. Often times, for example, inter-agency mechanisms, like other "building blocks", are set up at the agenda-setting stage already, and policy objectives may be set well before causal relationships are addressed. An illustrative example is provided at the end of each chapter, continuing from the example given in the previous one.

4.1 Setting up participatory, inter-agency mechanisms

Government policy managers, depending on the cross-cutting extent of a policy issue, may organize inter-agency committees or taskforces (which could already have been established during the agenda-setting stage) to accomplish policy formulation tasks collectively or independently, as the case may be. This is especially needed when an issue is first initiated in one sector but whose solutions require multi-sector efforts or exert impacts on other sectors. In many countries that are party to MEAs, for example, an inter-ministerial task force is typically established and charged with the responsibility for formulating options to implement the national commitments to these MEAs.

To secure political commitment to integrated policy formulation, policy managers may also want to secure the patronage of senior officials or opinion leaders in these inter-agency, multi-stakeholder mechanisms. In addition, policy managers should involve agencies responsible for policy implementation, monitoring and evaluation at this stage so as to hear their views on the operational practicality of the options to be explored. Formal procedures are, however, necessary to resolve conflicts that might arise from the operation of these mechanisms. In this regard, the level of independence of such mechanisms should also be established. Policy managers should keep such mechanisms in place throughout the policy process.

Ad hoc policy formulation mechanisms may be supported by long-standing and independent policy communities – networks of actors, governmental or non-governmental, with interest and expertise in a common policy area.[23] Members of a policy community adhere to certain core shared values even though they may disagree over details. Getting involved in these communities is critical for having particular views considered in policy formulation, because policy ideas are proposed, examined, debated, and reconfigured through interactions among their members. Policy ideas alive in policy communities but not examined thoroughly need not be on the government's agenda right away, thus policy managers may face less pressure and risks to act on those ideas immediately.

The International Panel on Climate Change (IPCC), for example, is a policy community at an inter-governmental level that relies on national expertise and conducts research and discussions in anticipation of climate change. "The role of the IPCC is to assess on a comprehensive, objective, open and transparent basis the scientific, technical and socio-economic information relevant to understanding the scientific basis of risk of human-induced climate change, its potential impacts and alternatives for adaptation and mitigation."[24] "Every summary for policymakers issued by the IPCC is approved, word by word, by representatives of each of more than 100 governments."[25]

At the national level, the National Reconciliation Commissions (NRCs) which have been established in a number of post-conflict countries such as South Africa, Ghana, and Thailand are also policy communities. These NRCs are typically led by former senior officials such as a Supreme Court Judge or former Prime Minister. They are usually charged with the responsibility to gather evidence and propose solutions to achieve reconciliation.

Many policy communities, however, tend to be closed to certain groups or ranks of individuals. But integrated policy formulation requires innovative ideas, which in turn require an operational modality that allows new actors and new ideas to enter into policy deliberations. Policy managers and formulators, are therefore advised to engage key stakeholders in such communities, especially those who are most vulnerable and directly affected by the problem at hand. Where constraints exist on membership, flexible arrangements may be devised such as extending the observer status to new actors or setting up an issue specific hotline for the public. Where government policy managers find it difficult to open up the policy formulation process, other members of the policy communities should take the initiative instead, with tacit support from the policy managers. In the meantime, policy managers and formulators must pay attention to the quality and substance of the participatory approach, including substantive and institutionalized participation of the most relevant and strategic stakeholders early on in a policy process (see Box 3.1 in the previous chapter). They also need to adequately budget for involving these stakeholders.

To reap the full benefits of policy communities, policy managers should facilitate open and continuous interactions among members of these communities. They could utilize workshops, conferences, surveys, and consultation sessions to enable policy community members to share information and policy ideas with each other. In addition, policy managers should involve non-governmental and government-supported think tanks that have specialized knowledge and skills with regard to a particular policy issue and its solutions. Their involvement may help bypass the institutional constraints that government experts sometimes face when trying to come up with innovative, integrated policy options.

Finally, policy managers should develop strategies to support knowledge creation through policy research. They should anticipate and coordinate research on emerging policy issues that are potentially critical but are not yet on the policy agenda. This will enable substantiated articulation of the issues and policy options when these issues have got onto the government agenda. It will reduce the incidents where policymakers have to rush to adopt an under-studied policy solution due to the time pressure associated with the sudden emergence of an issue.

4.2 Analysing the causes of a policy issue

A causality analysis – one of the analytical "building blocks" – is useful in many cases for making policy formulation in a targeted fashion. For example, a policy formulator can analyse deforestation by looking at several plausible causes of the problem. If the main contributing factor is insufficient law enforcement, the development of policy options can focus on enforcement mechanisms. But if the main root cause is land-use conflicts, the search for policy options may need to consider reforming land tenures. In such analyses, the policy initiator should identify the agents responsible for the root causes whenever possible.

The United Nations Common Country Assessment (CCA) and the United Nations Development Assistance Framework (UNDAF) require analysis that "identifies the manifestation of the problem – or its effect on people, and its underlying and root causes", "disaggregated as much as possible by sex, age, geographic area, and ethnicity, among others".[26] The guidelines for conducting such analysis, say that: a) immediate causes determine the current status of the problem; b) underlying causes are the consequence of policies, laws, and availability of resources; and c) root causes concern attitudes and behaviours at different levels, including the family, communities, and governments. In addition, some root causes for different problems may be common to several issues. Identifying these common causes – typically covering ESE dimensions – of multiple problems will increase the chance for integrated policy responses to generate multiple impacts.[27]

In analysing the causes of a problem, policy formulators and other analysts are advised to use models and collect empirical evidences. This will help enhance the logic and rigor of the analysis. The most well established model is the market model, which considers public problems as results of imbalances in supply of and demand for public goods and services. For example, the problem of overflowing waste can be analysed in terms of excessive demand for the environment as a sink, relative to the environment's capacity to supply the sink functions. Approximately, this model may help determine the "immediate causes".

The production model focuses on the role of the government. The same problem of waste, for example, can be analysed in terms of the government's failure to regulate waste disposal, provide waste treatment facilities, or promote reduced waste generation. Approximately, this model may help determine the "underlying causes".

An evolutionary model can be used to analyse a problem by focusing on the process or trends in which an issue becomes an established problem. Thus, the problem of too much waste can be analysed in terms of the lack of awareness and wasteful consumption habits. Approximately, this model may help determine the "root causes".

A combined use of these models in problem analysis is likely to provide a comprehensive picture of the causes of a problem and thus generate a comprehensive mix of policy options. Generally, the market model suggests the use of price mechanism as a major solution, the production model the use of regulatory measures, and the evolutionary model the use of persuasive measures, all may be needed in IP to address a problem.

In analysing root causes, it is also important to address the dynamics of the causes in order to ensure that policy options will keep pace with the evolving conditions. This requires the analysis of not only the baseline of the root causes, but also the trends of these causes, and the events and policies that are likely to affect the trends. In responding to climate change, for example, it will not be useful to consider only the existing level of fossil fuel consumption and its impacts on carbon emissions; the projected increase in energy demand, the continued reliance on fossil fuels, and the difficult to remove perverse fossil fuel subsidies, etc. must also be taken into account.

There are specific analytical tools under each of these models. In the market model, for example, a typical tool is the cost-benefit analysis to understand the financial motivations that are associated with a problem. At a macro-level, there is the Computable General Equilibrium (CGE) model that can trace the causal relations throughout an economy based on "input-output" techniques. There are also tools that help analyse environmental and social issues such as spatial modeling and surveys. A rather exhaustive collection of analytical tools can be found in an EC-sponsored web-book "Sustainability A-Test".[28]

Many analytical tools are also relevant to assessing and comparing policy options focusing on ESE implications during the decision-making stage (note that in the policy formulation stage the focus is on causality analysis of the issue and assessment of policy options based on political, financial, and administrative considerations). This will be covered in the next chapter. Basically, when choosing analytical tools, policy formulators are encouraged to consider: a) data requirements; b) the costs and time involved; c) ability to deal with uncertainties; and d) transparency of the analytical process and the outputs.[29]

Note that the agenda-setting stage may also benefit from using these models and tools (i.e. "building blocks") to make the case for the issue in question. In that situation, the analysis will focus on how the issue – if left unaddressed – would affect the ESE dimensions of SD, covering risks, threats, opportunities, cumulative effects, and feedback loops. For example, a causality analysis may help describe the implications of increased water shortage – which is the issue of concern – for economic growth, human health, and biodiversity.

4.3 Setting policy objectives*

On the basis of the root-cause analysis, the policy formulator should determine objectives for a potential policy solution. These objectives should respond specifically to the problem and the root causes. For the problem of climate change, as an illustration, a general objective can be "to reduce global warming" with average temperature as the indicator. At a specific level, the objective can be "to cut global CO_2 emissions by 20 per cent from the 1990 level by 2030", which uses the amount of emissions as an indicator. At an operational level, the objectives can be "to remove all subsidies for fossil fuels by 2020" and "to levy a tax of US$10 per tonne of CO_2 emitted". These objectives should guide the search for policy options. Box 4.2 describes the requirements for setting objectives and Box 4.3 describes three levels of objectives, both taken from the EC's Impact

---

* This section draws heavily on the EC's IA Guidelines.

Assessment Guidelines. Policy formulators can start developing objectives in either a bottom-up or top-down manner, but typically this involves a number of iterations until the different levels of objectives are consistent and respond to the policy problem to be addressed. They are also reminded that the three levels of objectives are not necessarily required for all IP situations and that objectives should be limited in number to avoid confusion. Finally, in developing objectives especially at the general level, policy formulators should check whether the contemplated objectives are consistent with other broad SD objectives of the society. Then policy managers and the prospective decision-makers should confirm and publicize the proposed policy objectives.

4.4 Developing policy options

Developing alternative solutions to a defined issue creates space for maximizing the synergies and

---

Box 4.2: Setting SMART objectives

Objectives should be:

Specific: Objectives should be precise and concrete enough not to be open to varying interpretations.

Measurable: Objectives should define a desired future state in measurable terms, so that it is possible to verify whether the objective has been achieved or not. Such objectives are either quantified or based on a combination of description and scoring scales.

Accepted: If objectives and target levels are to influence behaviour, they must be accepted, understood and interpreted similarly by all of those who are expected to take responsibility for achieving them.

Realistic: Objectives and target levels should be ambitious – setting an objective that only reflects the current level of achievement is not useful – but they should also be realistic so that those responsible see them as meaningful.

Time-dependent: Objectives and target levels remain vague if they are not related to a fixed date or time period.

Source: The EC IA Guidelines, p20

minimizing trade-offs among a society's multiple values.[30] In practice, however, the scope of feasible options may be limited. In the public sector, there is often a preference for incremental alternatives, which seek changes that are only marginally different from the status quo. This is so mainly because:
a) information on the consequences of comprehensive policies is more difficult to obtain and thus such alternatives are often labelled as "unproven"; and b) comprehensive policies involve higher risks for many policymakers. Policy formulators should, therefore, anticipate and prepare for difficulties when suggesting comprehensive policy options that seek fundamental changes from the status quo.

The anti-corruption agenda promoted by the World Bank, for example, seeks to achieve fundamental improvement in governance in its borrowing countries. Stringent criteria are attached to its development assistance to these countries. But this effort might have gone a little ahead of what many countries may be prepared to deal with, turning some of the borrowers away from the Bank to other sources of funds that have no requirements on good governance. This is not to say that the Bank's agenda on corruption is wrong; the issue is one of appropriate extent, sequence, and pace. In some cases, drastic policies may be indeed what are most needed, as in the case of climate change.

Policy formulators can consider three approaches to developing alternative policy solutions:

1. **Policy transfer** – policy formulators can develop options by learning from the effects of other policies – especially successful ones – that have been applied in other places or sectors at a similar administrative level dealing with similar type of issues. These transferable policies can usually be found in "best practices" manuals published by various governmental and non-governmental institutions. Adaptation is usually needed to suit the particular problem at hand. The sulphur emission trading mechanism, for example, was first introduced in the U.S. in the 1990s, and it has since been adopted in the EU for carbon.

2. **Government's toolbox** – policy formulators can consider the usual means that the government has to address public problems. These include taxes,

---

Box 4.3: Three levels of objectives

General objectives

These are the overall goals of a policy and are expressed in terms of its outcome or ultimate impact. If successful, the intervention should at least induce change in the direction of the general objective (knowing that reaching high-level objectives will usually depend on other factors). Progress towards general objectives will often be measured by global indicators.

Example

General objective = Promote economic development of rural areas.

Indicator = Rate of economic growth in rural areas

Specific objectives

These are the immediate objectives of the policy – the targets that first need to be reached in order for the General Objectives to be achieved. They are expressed in terms of the direct and short-term effects of the policy.

Example

Specific objective = Encourage economic activity in rural areas

Indicator = Number of new enterprises setting up in rural areas

Operational objectives

The Operational Objectives are normally expressed in terms of outputs – goods or services that the intervention should produce. The achievement of these objectives (or deliverables) is usually under the direct control of those managing the intervention and thus can be directly verified.

Example

Operational objective = Provide financial assistance to projects promoting new enterprises in rural areas

Indicator = Number of projects receiving financial assistance

Source: The EC IA Guidelines, p.21.

---

regulation, subsidies, grants, government service provision, budget for government agencies, information released from official sources, property rights, macroeconomic management, education and consultation, financing and contracting, and institutional reforms.[31] For example, the inability of the market to price the provision of clean air is often identified as a major cause of air pollution and taxes are often used to correct such a failure. This is the case with UK's first pollution tax introduced in August 2007, which charges luxury cars and 4x4s £25 a day for driving into city centres.[32]

3. **Policy innovation** – policy formulators can also identify options that have the potential to achieve multiple impacts. This is where the potential for policy integration is strongest. Imposing fossil fuel taxes coupled with removing employment related taxes, for example, could address both problems of carbon emissions and unemployment without having to change the overall fiscal situation. Apart from this bundling of policies and issues, they should also search for options that may lie outside of the government. Seeking private sector engagement in international payments for conserving globally significant ecosystems such as the habitats for endangered species, for example, can overcome the limited resources a government has to provide incentives for conservation.

Given the time and resource constraints, policy formulators are only able to analyse a limited number of alternatives thoroughly. They should, therefore, weed out policy options that are clearly infeasible.[33] A fundamental criterion for screening is political acceptability. A policy option, no matter how good in theory, may be infeasible because it cannot be expected to gain the approval necessary to legitimize and implement it. One of the options for addressing the issue of illegal immigrants, for example, is to grant full and immediate citizenship, but this is politically infeasible in many countries.

Policy formulators, however, should not consider political support as a statistic, given factor. They should seek to conduct good evidence-based analysis to generate the political support needed for pursuing particular policy options. The option to include Reduced Emission from Deforestation and Degradation (REDD) in climate discussions, for example, was excluded in previous Conference of Parties (COPs) to the UNFCCC. With good analysis of the evidence showing how REDD could contribute to reduced CO_2 emission and generate co-benefits for biodiversity, this option managed to get serious attention at the UNFCCC Bali conference in December 2007.

Other criteria for screening the options at this stage are administrative feasibility and cost-effectiveness. One of the policy options to address the issue of over-fishing, for example, is to allocate fishing permits and allow trading of the permits. This system, however, requires a strong institution to monitor the landing of fishing boats in multiple locations, which can be administratively quite demanding for many developing countries. A related consideration is the cost involved in achieving a given policy target. Other things being equal, an alternative that has the least financial cost (or achieving more with the same cost) should be favoured. To meet carbon reduction obligations, for example, businesses are able to either change their production processes directly or pay countries to plant trees to absorb carbon. The carbon market exists because for many businesses, paying others to offset their obligations is less costly.

Illustration: Formulating policy options for dealing with climate change

The IPCC, established in 1988, has served as a participatory and inter-governmental forum for developing and improving policy options. The IPCC was mandated to consider the need for:

- Identification of uncertainties and gaps in our present knowledge with regard to climate changes and its potential impacts, and preparation of a plan of action over the short-term in filling these gaps;

- Identification of information needed to evaluate policy implications of climate change and response strategies;

- Review of current or planned national/international policies related to greenhouse gas issues;

- Scientific and environmental assessments of all aspects of the greenhouse gas issue and the transfer of these assessments and other relevant information to governments and intergovernmental organizations to be taken into account in their policies on social and economic development and environmental programmes.

Over the past 20 years, the IPCC has conducted and collected voluminous analyses on the causes, trends, and potential impacts of climate change. It has also provided an analytical basis for setting a realistic policy objective for a global climate policy – "stabilization of greenhouse gas concentrations in the atmosphere at a level that would prevent dangerous anthropogenic interference with the climate system".[34]

Various policy options have been floated by the IPCC ranging from border tax adjustment for tradable products whose climate related negative external costs are not internalized, to Clean Development Mechanism (CDM) or Joint Implementation (JI) which support emission-reduction (or emission removal) projects in developing countries and transition economies. CDM and JIs allow countries or businesses to earn emission reduction units (ERUs) also called certified emission reduction (CER) credits, each equivalent to the reduction of one tonne of CO_2. The scope of CDM and JI projects includes energy, agriculture, waste handling, reduction of fugitive emission from fuels, etc. These mechanisms stimulate emission reductions, while giving industrialized countries some flexibility in how they meet their emission reduction targets.

Further reading

Bardach, Eugene. *A practical guide for policy analysis : the eightfold path to more effective problem solving.* New York: Chatham House Publishers, 2000

Howlett, M., and M. Ramesh. (2003) *Studying Public Policy: Policy Cycles and Policy Subsystems*, OUP.

Lester, Jame P. and Joseph Stewart (2000), Public policy: an evolutionary approach, Belmont, Calif.: Wadsworth.

MacRae, D. and D. Whittington. (1997) Expert Advice for Policy Choice: Analysis and Discourse. Washington DC: Georgetown University Press, 1997.

Putt, A. and J. Springer (1989).*Policy Research: Concepts, Methods, and Applications,* Prentice Hall.

Weimer, D. and A. Vining (1992), *Policy Analysis: Concepts and Practice,* Prentice Hall.

References

21. Howlett, M, and M. Ramesh. (2003) Studying Public Policy: Policy Cycles and Policy Subsystems, Oxford University Press.

22. Lester, Jame P. and Joseph Stewart (2000), Public policy: an evolutionary approach, Belmont, Calif.: Wadsworth, 2000

23. Baumgartner, F. R. and B. D. Jones (1991). "Agenda Dynamics and Policy Subsystems." Journal of Politics 53(4): 1044-1074.

24. Intergovernmental Panel on Climate Change (IPCC). (1988). About IPCC. Retrieved March 2009 from http://www.ipcc.ch/about/index.htm

25. Field, C. (2007). States have right to challenge IPCC climate reports. Retrieved March 2009 from http://search.ft.com/ftArticle?queryText =IPCC&taje=false&tid=070807000772&ct=0

26. United Nations. (2007). Common Country Assessment and United Nations Development Assistance Framework. Retrieved March 2009 from http://www.undg.org/docs/6860/ 2007%20CCA%20and%20UNDAF%20 Guidelines%20FINAL.doc

27. http://www.undp.org/policy/docs/ UNDG_UNCT_PRSP.pdf

28. IVM. (2006). Advanced Tools for Sustainability Assessment: The Sustainability A-Test. Retrieved March 2009 from http://ivm5.ivm.vu.nl/sat/

29. UNEP, Integrated Assessment and Planning for Sustainable Development: Key features, steps, and tools, Version 1, April 2005. p8.

30. MacRae, D. and D. Whittington. (1997) Expert Advice for Policy Choice: Analysis and Discourse. Washington DC: Georgetown University Press, 1997.

31. E. Bardach.

32. *The Daily Mail* (2007). Luxury cars to be charged £25 tax under Britain's first pollution tax. Retrieved June 2009 from http://www.dailymail.co.uk/news/ article-473330/Luxury-cars-charged-25-tax-Britains-pollution-tax.html

33. Bardach, Eugene. A practical guide for policy analysis : the eightfold path to more effective problem solving. New York: Chatham House Publishers, 2000.

34. UNFCCC. (1994). Article 2: Objectives. Retrieved February 2009 from http://unfccc.int/essential_background/ convention/background/items/1353.php

* Extracts from the IPCC 10th Year Anniversary Brochure http://www.ipcc.ch/pdf/10th-anniversary/anniversary-brochure.pdf

5. Decision-making

Decision-making is not synonymous with policymaking. In public policy sciences, decision-making is described as a stage where a government decision-maker or an official decision-making body selects a course of action or non-action among a small set of policy options identified at the policy formulation stage with a view towards policy implementation. It is highly political because decisions often create winners and losers even if the decision is to do nothing and to retain the status quo. It can also be highly technical because of the complexities involved in assessing and comparing policy options based on their projected ESE consequences, the basis on which an integrated decision is supposed to be made.

The list of actors with the authority to make decisions varies across countries and sectors, but it typically includes heads of government agencies directly responsible for the problem area, legislators if legislative approval for the decision is required, and the judiciary if the constitutionality of the decision is to be verified. Various interest groups are also involved in decision-making through lobbying activities directed at influencing decision-makers. In some instances, the public is able to have their say on a decision through their participation in referenda.

Decision-making – Key points

Choose criteria for decision-making

- Choose criteria in alignment with significant ESE dimensions: economic efficiency, social equity, and environmental friendliness in addition to participatory process.

- Select one or more critical indicators for each criterion based on national or local circumstances, including a time span, and ensuring that the indicators are highly communicative, creditable, and for which data are available or could be collected at a reasonable cost.

Establish a baseline

- Include a "business as usual" scenario, which implies a policy option of "no action".

- Collect information on current conditions, current and expected trends, and effects of other related policies, all of which are compared to established indicators.

Assess and compare policy options

- Use various "building blocks" of analytical tools to project the sustainable development implications of each option in relation to established indicators.

- Avoid biases towards quantitative indicators, positive impacts, or a single dimension of SD.

- Focus progressively on the most significant ESE impacts.

- Organize and compare the results of assessment in a decision-matrix in a highly communicative and transparent form.

- Highlight win-win opportunities as well as inevitable trade-offs and propose additional measures to strengthen synergies or minimize trade-offs.

Making an informed decision

- Decide on a policy option that maximizes synergies and minimizes trade-offs in an ideal situation.

- Make it hard to reject a win-win option or to adopt a worst option through sound assessment, public communication, as well as transparency and accountability requirements for decision-makers.

Analysts and issue-specific experts can play a vital, albeit indirect, role in decision-making by providing information and analysis to decision-makers. They can be affiliated with key decision-makers, external agencies, and social actors as their staff or consultants, or they may work independently. To enhance analytical quality and encourage policy innovation, government policy managers and decision-makers can promote competing assessments of policy options, especially by independent analysts or research institutions to avoid sectoral biases. This will help reduce the risks of having assessments hijacked by narrowly defined organizational and personal interests. External agencies can also sponsor assessment efforts that are integral parts of a policy process.

This chapter describes how SD considerations, which have been carried through agenda-setting and policy formulation stages, can advance into the decision-making stage. It focuses on four steps: a) choosing decision criteria; b) establishing a baseline; c) assessing and comparing the ESE implications of policy options identified at the policy formulation stage; and d) making an informed decision.

It should be noted that a participatory process is encouraged to run throughout the entire policy process. Since this "building block" is already described under "agenda-setting" and "implementation" stages, this chapter will not cover this important aspect specifically, even though it is also fundamental to the decision-making stage.

5.1 Choosing decision criteria

Government decision-makers make decisions to advance objectives that are of value to society. They need to set criteria to judge whether or not the consequences of a decision are indeed valuable to society.[35] In addition, they need to use the same criteria for comparing different policy options to ensure consistency. There could be many criteria, but from an SD perspective, the most essential categories for assessing the consequences of policy options may include: economic efficiency, social equity, environmental friendliness, and participatory process, as detailed below. Specific values or standards for these criteria, of course, may differ from society to society.

Economic efficiency: achieving a given policy objective (solving a policy problem or realizing a public benefit) at the minimal cost or maximizing the value of the objective at a given cost.

Social equity: achieving a given objective in a way that conforms to a society's shared sense of fairness and human rights, especially with regard to the poor and marginalized segments of society, including women, children, and future generations.

Environmental friendliness: achieving a given objective in a way that conforms to domestic and international environmental laws and standards.

Participatory process: achieving a given objective in a consultative, transparent, and accountable manner.

Adopting these criteria implies assessing the ESE implications of policy options, a subject well studied under the various sustainability-oriented assessment activities. It will enable decision-makers to explore synergistic opportunities among different dimensions of SD, identify trade-offs if any, demand mitigation measures to minimize trade-offs, and ensure consistency across public policies of different sectors and agencies.

Establishing these criteria is another "building block", which can be applied much earlier in a policy process or independently from any particular policy process. To encourage system-wide application of an integrated approach to public policy, for example, a top level government agency may want to formally require the adoption of the above-mentioned criteria for decision-making in the public sector across the board. This should be followed by capacity building efforts to enable sectoral agencies to consider impacts that are typically beyond their areas of concern. This "building block" is covered in this particular chapter because of the logical proximity between criteria-setting and decision-making.

Moreover, criteria provide a broad scope within which policy options may be considered and compared. Each criterion still requires an indicator or a number of indicators that are specific to the policy situation and can be measured to show whether that particular criterion is satisfied or not. Under the economic efficiency criterion, for example, an indicator could be the total monetary cost of implementing a policy option (e.g. phasing out particular Persistent Organic Substances as required by the Stockholm Convention) as a percentage of the Gross Domestic Product (GDP). International organizations have invested a lot in the work on SD indicators over the last two decades. They are in a good position to share the related knowledge and experiences.

Policy formulators should select indicators that can be communicated effectively and credibly to decision-makers and the public and for which the data are expected to be available or can be collected at a reasonable cost. Merely reporting pollution levels, for example, may not capture the decision-makers' and the public's attention to the pollution's severity unless these levels are related to how they affect society and human life, such as productivity and human health and how a particular decision can reduce such harms.

5.2 Establishing a baseline

A "baseline", also referred to as a "business as usual" scenario, describes what would happen to established indicators if there were no change in government decisions and if existing trends were to continue.[36] Note that this baseline is different from the status quo because there can be changes from the status quo due to naturally occurring events and effects of other policies. The time span for a baseline assessment should be the same as used to assess other policy options.

Because a baseline is different from the status quo, collecting the information necessary for establishing the baseline is technically challenging and time-consuming. The following information compared with established indicators is required to obtain a baseline for assessment: a) current conditions (or status quo); b) current and expected trends; c) effects of policies being implemented; and d) effects of other foreseeable policies.

The baseline provides an essential reference point against which various other policy options can be compared. Without the baseline, the option of "let present trends continue" is automatically dropped out of consideration, leaving the door open for policy interventions that might aggravate policy problems. Sometimes poorly designed policies can be worse than no policy.

The flip side of this is of course the bias towards no action. While there are risks from policy changes and

the results may be uncertain, the same is true of maintaining the status quo, whose future is also uncertain and may also have risks. Lack of this recognition is one of the causes of resistance to change. There is the assumption that the future will be like the past, despite a whole history of disproof.

5.3 Assessing ESE implications of policy options

Assessment during the decision-making stage of IP aims at revealing the direction, magnitude, duration, and reversibility of changes that may result from each policy option under consideration. The most challenging aspect of assessment is projecting the future, which is inherently uncertain, despite the availability of various "building blocks" tools and techniques.

Many tools and techniques are available for assessing the implications of policy options against SD criteria and indicators. Cost-effective analysis, cost-benefit analysis, and CGE models, for example, have been used to measure the economic efficiency of policy options, surveys to gauge the potential equity implications, and ecological and spatial modelling to depict environmental changes. These "building blocks" or tools can be applied for a variety of purposes, not only for causal analysis of the issue in question and financial feasibility analysis at the policy formulation stage, but also for projecting the ESE implications of policy options at the decision-making stage. A comprehensive collection of analytical tools can be found in the EC-sponsored web-book "Sustainability A-Test".[37] What is typically missing, however, is the application of system tools and techniques that consider the interactions across the ESE domains over a long-period of time, beyond 5-10 years, a major characteristic of SD concerns.

When applying assessment tools, policy formulators and decision-makers should be cautious against the following biases:

- A bias towards indicators for which quantitative measures are available. Some impacts may not be quantifiable because of data gaps despite their vital importance. Qualitative measures of these impacts can be developed based on judgement informed by experience and knowledge.

- A bias towards positive impacts or potential opportunities. Both positive impacts (opportunities) and negative impacts (risks) are critical in assessing policy options, and overlooking negative impacts may lead to wrong decisions.

- A bias towards impacts of a particular dimension closely associated with the identity of the organization conducting the assessment.

The EC proposed three progressive steps to assess the intended and unintended ESE impacts of a policy option against multiple criteria:

1. Make a broad judgement on the range of ESE impacts including general causalities, the extent of the impacts, which groups will be affected, over what time period, and how the existing inequalities will be affected;

2. On the basis of the first step, identify the most critical impacts based on causal models, qualitative assessment of the likelihoods, magnitudes, and importance of the impacts, or an impact matrix connecting specific policy components (usually expressed as "measures") with critical impacts on key areas of concern; and

3. Building on the previous steps, conduct an in-depth analysis of selected critical impacts in either qualitative or quantitative terms or both.[38]

Establishing a benchmark and assessing projected impacts can generate an immense amount of information and, therefore, there is a need to systematize its collection and display. A convenient way to organize information in a systematic way is to display it in the form of a decision matrix (see Table 5.1).

A typical decision matrix arrays policy options down the rows and decision criteria/indicators across the columns. Any cell in the decision matrix contains the projected outcome of the policy option as assessed by reference to the column for criterion/indicators. For example, Cell A1 contains information on the outcome of Option A as assessed by reference to Criterion 1/Indicator 1.

In IP, the general criteria in the decision matrix can be aligned along the ESE dimensions. Each of these criteria can be reflected through one or a number of indicators, which can be qualitative, quantitative, or in monetary terms. The EC's IA Guidelines provided more elaborated examples of different ways to compare policy options and display the results in a transparent and accessible manner.[39]

To aid decision-making, each option in the matrix should be linked to each criterion and its indicators systematically. This can be accomplished by

Table 5.1: Decision Matrix

Criteria	Option A	Option B	Option C	Option.....
Criterion 1 Indicator 1 Indicator 2 Indicator...	A1	B1	C1	...
Criterion 2 Indicator 1 Indicator 2 Indicator...	A2	B2	C2	...
Criterion 3 Indicator 1 Indicator 2 Indicator...	A3	B3	C3	...
Criteria ... Indicator 1 Indicator 2 Indicator...	A...	B...	C...	...

considering all cells, which can counter the biases of the analyst. Box 5.1 shows an example of decision matrices in practice.

As shown in Box 5.1, development need not come at the expense of the environment. Although total GDP for Papua in 2020 under Alternative D would be less than under Alternative B (the highest among the 4 scenarios), locally retained GDP, however, would be higher under D. In addition, D would create the highest number of jobs, retain the largest tract of forestland, and incur less government debt.

The comparison of policy options is relatively straightforward when one policy option is ranked the best according to all criteria, as in the example below. However, this should be considered as an exception rather than the norm because of the potential conflicts among different criteria. Trade-offs may be inevitable in some cases. Box 5.2 summarizes the basic rules in dealing with trade-offs.[40]

Assessing and comparing policy options provides opportunities for seeking win-win situations and minimizing trade-offs. Components in different alternatives can be reconfigured into a new alternative that may lead to win-win outcomes. Mitigation strategies can be developed to reduce any negative impacts or risks of options that are preferable according to most criteria. In this regard, the OECD DAC SEA Guidance provided a simple rule of thumb to deal with negative impacts: "first avoid; second reduce; and third off-set adverse impacts – using appropriate measures."[41]

Box 5.1: Comparative Assessment of Development Options in Papua, Indonesia

Papua is Indonesia's largest province endowed with dense tropical rainforest and many other natural resources, but its small population is among the poorest of all Indonesian provinces. At the beginning of the new millennium, the provincial government and local stakeholders identified a number of development alternatives: a) develop a mega-dam project (B); b) invest in a province-wide highway (C); and c) focus the development in existing urban centers (D). In 2002, local and international policy analysts, with the assistance of a system dynamics modeling tool, compared the outcomes (projected till 2020) of these alternatives plus the alternative of "business as usual", as illustrated in the following decision matrix:

Criteria/Indicators	2000 Value	Business-as-Usual (A)	Dam (B)	Highway (C)	Urban (D)
Economic					
Papua GDP (in 1993 Rp billion)	8,478	19,076	23,068	19,621	394,048
Locally Retained GDP (in 1993 Rp billion	3	7,020	7,120	7,084	7,799
Environment					
Forestland (million hectares)	23	16	13	8	17
Pollution index	1.07	1.67	2.01	1.73	1.75
Social					
Total employment (persons, thousands)	913	1,065	1,212	1,099	1,310

Source: Sheng, Fulai, CCG Report – Comparative Assessment of Development Options, Center for Conservation and Government at Conservation International (2004), pg 19 – 21.

5.4 Making an informed decision

Ideally, decision-makers should adopt a policy option that solves the problem in a way that maximizes synergies and minimizes trade-offs among different societal imperatives. But this assumes that the consequences of each policy option can be known in advance. In reality, however, the consequences of various policy options are rarely known with certainty, the time to make policy comparisons is often lacking, and decisions are rarely made by a single decision-maker.

To overcome these limitations, policy initiators, policy formulators, and decision-makers – with the support from external agencies if needed and appropriate – are advised to invest in raising analytical capacity, gathering good data and information, and using new information technologies and analytical tools, to support "good enough" decisions.

But even if an assessment is as comprehensive and integrated as it can be, it is but one input – albeit a quite significant one – for decision-making. A final decision can be made against a policy option that is ranked best in all dimensions. Political imperatives, narrowly defined agency interests, and decision-makers' self interests can overrule what appears to be the most "sustainable" or "integrated" decision. The final decision is often the outcome of strategic interaction, bargaining, and compromise among multiple decision-makers as it is rare to have only a sole, unitary decision-maker responsible for arriving at a decision.

The highly political nature of making decisions, however, does not imply that the value of sound assessment should be discounted. The assessment can effectively set a boundary within which trade-offs can be made between political imperatives and technical merits. For example, it is much easier to reject the worst policy option when its negative impacts or risk are conclusively indicated by the assessment. By the same token, it creates a tremendous hurdle for decision-makers to ignore a win-win solution. In this regard, effective public communication of the results from comparing policy options may play a significant role in mobilizing public opinions and tilting decisions towards synergistic policy options.

Placing accountability and transparency requirements on decision-makers will also reinforce the power of sound assessment in

---

Box 5.2: Rules on making trade-offs

- Any trade-off must deliver maximum net gains

- The burden of argument for trade-off should be on the trade-off proponent

- Significant adverse effects must be avoided

- The future should be given at least the same weight as the present

- All trade-offs must be accompanied by explicit justification

- Decisions on trade-offs must be made through an open process

Source: Based on R.B. Gibson et al (2005)

---

support of IP. The United Nations Development Programme (UNDP) broadly defines accountability to mean "holding individuals and organizations responsible for performance measured as objectively as possible" and transparency to mean "all means of facilitating the citizen's access to information and also his/her understanding of decision-making mechanisms". UNDP states that "accountability and transparency are indispensable pillars of good governance that compel the state, private sector and civil society to focus on results, seek clear objectives, develop effective strategies, and monitor and report on performance. Through public accountability and transparency, governments (together with civil society and the private sector) can achieve congruence between public policy, its implementation and the efficient allocation of resources." [42]

Things will get more complicated for decision-making when trade-offs among different interests are inevitable. Sound assessment, however, is still of great value to enhance the quality of a decision. It forces decision-makers to openly share their values with other stakeholders or the general public when decisions are made, employing transparency and accountability that might elude the public otherwise. More important, better information about various policy options enables stakeholders and the public to substantively participate in the policy process.

Illustration: Deciding on climate policy options

At the Rio Earth Summit in 1992 the United Nations Framework Convention on Climate Change (UNFCCC) was open for signature. In 1994, the UNFCCC entered into force. In December 1997, the Kyoto Protocol to the UNFCCC was adopted and it came into force in 2005 after seven years of negotiations involving over 160 countries. In this long process leading to the decision on the Kyoto Protocol, which is an operational document under the UNFCCC, the baseline for global temperature and for GHG emission reduction by developed countries was established in 1990. A fundamental criterion for deciding on policy options is the principle of "common but differentiated responsibilities" among different groups of countries. [43]

Assessing and comparing the various policy options against this criterion and other criteria such as the principles of international law, the States' sovereign right to exploit their own resources pursuant to their own environmental and developmental policies, and cost-effectiveness, the Parties to the UNFCCC agreed on the following three market-based policy options:

- Emissions trading – countries that have a surplus in their allowed emission units can sell the excess to countries that have a deficit.[44]

- Clean Development Mechanism – a developed country obligated to reduce emissions can implement an emission-reduction project in developing countries, which can count towards their obligations.[45]

- Joint implementation – a developed country or a transition economy earns emission reduction units (ERUs) from an emission-reduction or emission removal project in another country of the same category, each ERU being equivalent to one tonne of CO_2, which can count towards its Kyoto obligation.[46]

Further Reading

Bardach, Eugene. A practical guide for policy analysis : the eightfold path to more effective problem solving. New York: Chatham House Publishers, 2000

Howlett, M, and M. Ramesh. (2003) Studying Public Policy: Policy Cycles and Policy Subsystems, Oxford University Press.

Lester, Jame P. and Joseph Stewart (2000), Public policy: an evolutionary approach, Belmont, Calif.: Wadsworth, 2000

MacRae, D. and D. Whittington. (1997) Expert Advice for Policy Choice: Analysis and Discourse. Washington DC: Georgetown University Press, 1997

Patton, C and Sawicki, D (1996), Basic Methods of Policy Analysis and Planning, Essex: Prentice Hall/Harvester Wheatsheaf.

Putt, A. and J. Springer (1989). *Policy Research: Concepts, Methods, and Applications*, Prentice Hall.

Quade, E.S. (1989), *Analysis for Public Decisions*, Elsevier Science, New York, NY

Weimer, D. and A. Vining (1992), *Policy Analysis: Concepts and Practice*, Prentice Hall

References

35. The EC IA Guidelines, p20.

36. Bardach, Eugene. A practical guide for policy analysis : the eightfold path to more effective problem solving. New York: Chatham House Publishers, 2000.

37. IVM. (2006). Advanced Tools for Sustainability Assessment: The Sustainability A-Test. Retrieved March 2009 from http://ivm5.ivm.vu.nl/sat/

38. The EC IA Guidelines, p27-36.

39. The EC IA Guidelines 39-43.

40. R.B. Gibson, et al, Sustainability Assessment: Criteria and Processes, Earthscan, 2005. pp.139-140.

41. OECD DAC SEA Guidance, p58.

42. UNDP, "Accountability Transparency Integrity".

43. UNFCCC. (1998). The Kyoto Protocol to the UNFCCC. Retrieved February 2009 from http://unfccc.int/resource/docs/convkp/kpeng.pdf

44. UNFCCC. (n.d.). Emissions Trading. Retrieved February 2009 from http://unfccc.int/kyoto_protocol/mechanisms/emissions_trading/items/2731.php

45. UNFCCC. (n.d.). Clean Development Mechanism. Retrieved February 2009 from http://unfccc.int/kyoto_protocol/mechanisms/clean_development_mechanism/items/2718.php

46. UNFCCC. (n.d.). Joint Implementation. Retrieved February 2009 from http://unfccc.int/kyoto_protocol/mechanisms/joint_implementation/items/1674.php

6. Implementation

Implementation is the stage where a selected policy option must be translated into action. It is probably the most difficult, demanding, and critical stage in a policy process. Any deficiency in policy design or any vulnerability with respect to the policy environment will become visible at this stage. Yet implementation is often neglected in practice. Policy managers, initiators, formulators, decision-makers, and others involved in the policy process often fail to systematically prepare the ground for implementation, resulting in policies that perform far below expectation or even policy disasters. Despite over 500 MEAs, for example, there has been little sign of environmental improvement and some problems such as climate change have escalated to the level of crisis.[47]

One reason for this neglect is the sheer complexity, both analytical and practical, that implementation poses. Another reason is the political sensitivity

---

Implementation – Key points

Considering implementation challenges throughout the policy cycle

- Sequence policy measures strategically when formulating policy options by starting small to allow quick results, alliance building, and policy learning.
- Review the logical construction systematically prior to implementation to ensure that policy "inputs" have a reasonable chance to produce policy "outputs".
- Carry out tasks strategic to implementation early on: a) build a constituency supportive of policy change; b) set overall objectives for policy; and c) secure sufficient formal authorization and resource for the policy process.

Getting organized and operational fast

- Designate an inter-sectoral, inter-agency mechanism to be responsible for implementation, which can build on mechanisms established earlier in the policy process.
- Clarify roles and mandates of all the participants involved in the implementation mechanism.
- Identify individuals and units within organizations, including the non-governmental sector, to implement adopted policy measures.
- Translate broad policy objectives into operational targets and tasks linked to individuals and units and tied to budgets.
- Use Results-Based Management to guide operational planning and ensure that the capacity, incentives, and positive inter-personal relationships are in place for successful implementation.

Mobilizing resources proactively

- Consider resource mobilization a constant challenge rather than a one-off task.
- Seek short-term seed funds as appropriate to demonstrate initial success while securing stable sources of funding for the long term.

Managing stakeholder dynamics

- Conduct a stakeholder analysis, which should and could be done in an earlier stage, covering those who are potentially concerned by, interested in, important to, or having any power over the policy being initiated.
- Consider different stakeholders' interests, level of organization, resources and capacities, and options for action.
- Support the participation of vulnerable groups and guard against powerful groups capturing the policy process.

associated with implementation. In policy formulation and even decision-making, critical differences between stakeholders may be papered over by using vague language or even postponing decisions on mission-critical but politically or bureaucratically "sensitive" aspects of policies outright. This has the advantage of keeping a policy process moving forward and "buying time" for more supportive coalitions to be built. But the consequences of such avoidance become unavoidable during the implementation stage, in which those tasked with implementation will struggle to generate, allocate, and control resources and interpret policy intentions as the intended outputs and results of a policy fail to materialize or as negative side-effects of policies become evident.

The high degree of diversity among stakeholders involved in IP increases the complexity and vulnerability of implementation. Implementation creates winners and losers. It is the stage where the stakes of winning or losing begin to manifest themselves clearly to participants who have been left out of the earlier stages in the process. Most organizations may resist coordination due to a perceived threat to autonomy or disagreements over the nature of the tasks being pursued. Agencies and even divisions within agencies may compete for resources and control. Clashes may also occur among the public, private, non-profit, and community sectors.

Thus, the stakes in "getting implementation right" – in designing interventions that make successful implementation more likely and in anticipating and building in mechanisms to overcome implementation difficulties – are particularly high. Policy managers, initiators, formulators, decision-makers, implementers, and other policy participants interested in IP must, therefore, bring implementation problems into their consideration from the onset.

This chapter describes how policies, after having been subject to the rigorous SD "filtering" so far, can receive a chance to be implemented and achieve integration on the ground. It focuses on four aspects: 1) considering implementation when formulating policies and making decisions; 2) getting specific and operational fast; 3) mobilizing resources proactively for implementation; and 4) managing stakeholder dynamics.

6.1 Considering implementation challenges throughout a policy process

Policy change is a dynamic, non-linear process. It rarely involves a straightforward mobilization of the resources necessary to achieve well defined policy objectives that already have broad support. Instead, the implementation task can and often does involve elements of all the preceding policymaking stages. For example, it may involve re-interpretation and re-negotiation of policy objectives and may find implementers re-making decisions among significantly different options that may affect the type of policy outcomes actually produced. Table 6.1 summarizes the major implementation challenges, many of which are also applicable to other stages of IP.

Implementation considerations should, therefore, be incorporated directly into the design stage of any policy. One way to do this is to sequence policy measures strategically. Starting small while building constituencies for ambitious interventions is often warranted where policies are contested or facing uncertain prospects due to incomplete information. There are a range of unknowns at the onset of any policy process, not least regarding the incentives faced by, and inclinations of, different actors who must work together during implementation. Thus, conceiving small-scale initiatives as "policy experiments"[48] can help facilitate adaptive implementation – the ability to learn what works, and how to fix what isn't working – in the very process of implementation. The design of policy experiments requires, however, the existence of strong information and monitoring systems, a point reinforced in the following chapter.

Another key to the proper design of a policy from an implementation perspective is to systematically review its logical construction prior to the implementation stage. Policy managers, formulators, and implementers should test the degree to which a policy is logically constructed so that invested inputs stand a realistic chance of being processed into project-level outputs, which in turn contribute reliably to policy outcomes of interest. "Forward" and "Backward Mapping" are tools that may help ensure that policies are logically and soundly designed to achieve their stated objectives and that all the elements required for implementation are "assembled" and in place (see Box 6.1).

Table 6.1 Typical implementation barriers

Problem	Description in IP context
Support and authorization barriers	
Slow authorization	Operational plans and resource mobilization proceed slowly due to multiple veto points, making progress difficult.
Weak political support	Operational plans may proceed and even attain moderate success in the initial phase while flying under the "radar" of key politicians with opposing interests, until the plans begin to "scale up"
Bureaucratic opposition	Key players in the inter-agency network slow or sabotage implementation due to low priority of IP approach, lacking incentives, and/or competing interests.
Poor incentives for implementer	Local implementers (local government coordinating executives or front-line staff of agencies) who were not consulted during the earlier stages of IP have inadequate "buy-in" or incentives to comply with directives from the top.
Analytical competence barriers	
Vague or multiple missions	Inter-sectoral nature of policies and implementation leads to papering over conflicting goals or not clearly specifying trade-offs in operational terms during the earlier stages
Changing priorities	Decisions may need to be reconsidered in light of changing conditions.
Poor design	Integrated policies are complex and prone to poor design. If any of the complexities are left unaddressed, failure is pre-determined.
Uneven feasibility	Different components of the integrated policy may be operationally linked – one can only advance if another is present – subjecting operations to the "weakest link".
Operational capacity barriers	
Funding limitations	Funds necessary to implement approved operational plans are slow to materialize, blocking progress while key elements of situation change "facts on the ground" and/or initial supporters of the effort lose heart and abandon effort.
Weak management structure or network coordination capacity	Poor precedents for, or lacking history of, coordination between major agencies – exacerbated in case of inter-sectoral partnerships – makes routine operational decisions slow and implementation dysfunctional.
Lack of clarity in operational plans	Approved and funded operational plans are mismanaged due to poor specification of roles, responsibilities, and accountability. Often made worse by poor oversight and information systems with which to hold implementers accountable and make course corrections.

Implementation tasks are, however, not confined to the policy formulation stage. These tasks are understood as "a continuum of strategic and operational tasks"[49] (see table 6.2). Strategic tasks relate to the highest levels of policy formulation and overall responsibility for implementation. They overlap considerably across policymaking stages and include: 1) build constituencies supportive of policy change among a range of stakeholders, who bring different resources and interests to the table; 2) set overall objectives and design critical parameters for policies; and 3) at some point, secure sufficient formal authorization and resources necessary to drive the process forward.

The implementation of programmes, plans, and projects – i.e. the sub-components of a particular policy – has a more restricted focus and is more concrete, i.e. "operational". At this level, the tasks include: 1) identify individuals and units within organizations including in the non-governmental sector that will carry forward specific plans and collaborations; 2) operationalize policy objectives into specific, measurable targets that are in turn broken down into supporting tasks to be implemented by identifiable groups of people on a schedule; and 3) ensure necessary operational capacity, including attention not just to equipment and human resources but also to the incentives for grassroots implementers to act as required for successful execution of the policy intention.

All these tasks can be mapped onto the overarching IP framework presented in Chapter 2 (see Figure 6.1). Tasks related to implementation are integrated throughout the diagram, beginning from high-level "strategic" design considerations to operational-level design and capacity building tasks in later stages of the policy process. Although there are sequential aspects to the framework (describing a logical progression from agenda-setting to evaluation), a key message is that to be effective, implementation considerations must be reflected throughout the policy process. Failing this, large gaps are likely to loom between policy intentions and actual execution.

6.2 Get organized and operational fast

An essential part of the implementation stage is the designation of an institution to be charged with the overall responsibility for implementation. Typically, however, no single agency can be fully responsible for implementation of an integrated policy. Thus, an inter-sectoral, inter-agency mechanism – building on existing mechanism as much as possible – is often

---

Box 6.1: Forward and Backward Mapping

In forward mapping, the policy manager or formulator writes out (for her- or himself) how implementation is implicitly supposed to take place (if it is to be successful), including all the relevant actors, their roles, and the sequence and orchestration of their actions. S/he then uses this narrative as the basis for two fundamental critiques: is each of the actors actually likely to be sufficiently incentivized and capable of acting in the manner prescribed (critique 1)?; and might any other actor affected by the policy get involved to potentially interfere or deflect policy intentions during implementation, and (if so), can they actually be stopped from doing so (critique 2)? Based on the answers to these questions, s/he then rewrites the scenario to make it more realistic, including preventive and other measures to enhance the likelihood of success given this form of stakeholder analysis.

Backward mapping involves first specifying the actual behaviours that need to take place in order for policy outcomes to be achieved. For instance, in order to achieve the policy goal of cleaning up city canals, one might specify the behavioural change that "city inhabitants no longer throw their garbage into the canal". Having laid out such specific behaviours to be changed, the policy manager or formulator then designs policies from among different logical options that can help achieve this objective, paying special attention to how the intervention can practically motivate the required changes in behaviour.

These analytical tools are in some ways quite common-sensical and straightforward. But they may prove surprisingly useful in anticipating policy implementation problems, and in brainstorming alternative policy options to increase the likelihood of implementation success.

Source: Weimar and Vining, p. 402-406

Table 6.2: Implementation: a continuum of strategic and operational tasks

Policy implementation (emphasis on strategic tasks)	Programme/plan implementation	Project implementation (emphasis on operational tasks)
■ Constituency building ■ Overall policy objective-setting and design ■ Designing the implementation framework – overall responsibilities and resource allocations to different actors ■ Legitimization ■ Resource mobilization	■ Programme design ■ Capacity building for implementers ■ Collaboration with multiple groups and organizations ■ Expanding resources and support ■ Active leadership	■ Clear objectives ■ Defined roles and responsibilities ■ Plans/schedules ■ Rewards and sanctions ■ Feedback/adaptation mechanisms

Source: adapted from Table 2.1 in Brinkerhoff and Crosby (2002), p. 25.

needed to implement policies collectively. An important criterion for such a mechanism is the extent to which a network of actors interacts constructively to produce agreed policy outcomes. Mechanisms established in earlier stages of the policy cycle may well evolve to assume the implementation mandate. In this context, four types of intersectoral, interagency groupings may be identified:

- Overall coordinating committees officially designated with policy formulation and decision-making responsibilities in a particular issue area;

- Formal teams who guide implementation and operations – the direct "managers" or "operational coordinators" of an implementation process;

- Ad hoc working groups convened to solve specific management problems; and

- Stakeholder workshops convened to review and solicit feedback from stakeholders, in multiple communities or jurisdictions, affected by a policy.[50]

These groupings may have largely overlapping institutional membership but vary in the management level of the individuals staffing it. Regardless of the specific membership, however, policy managers should clarify, to the extent practical, the roles and mandates of these various steering and implementation teams, their relationship to more permanent authorities (political and bureaucratic), and the resources – legal, financial and bureaucratic – that they may draw on in

executing their respective responsibilities. At the same time, policy managers should expect that any authority may be contested in practice, prior to or during implementation. Policy managers are advised to use the steering committees as forums for resolving inevitable interagency and even intersectoral conflicts, rather than trying to avoid them altogether.

Apart from designating an overall institution responsible for implementation, there is also a need for operational planning – a process of developing initial and intermediate outputs and implementation targets for the interrelated programmes and projects that may contribute to policy objectives in a particular setting. Tasks need to be linked with specific institutions, including non-governmental entities, and if possible individuals, as well as financial resources. Implementation guidelines necessary for interpreting policies are also typically required. Results-Based Management is a popular tool that can assist in operational planning (see Box 6.2). In general, the more quickly implementers can move into operational planning, the higher the likelihood of successful execution. Quick results are often necessary to sustain coalition-building momentum as a policy initiative shifts gear from initial, smaller interventions and projects to larger, more integrated, inter-sectoral plans, programmes, and policies.

Policy managers can allocate implementation tasks to a special task force, an existing agency to

Figure 6.1: Implementation tasks, resources and analytical aids

Implementation tasks

- Modifying organizational structures
- Identifying network capacities necessary for implementation
- Developing concrete plans, performance expectations and accountability, creating and carrying out of do-able activities

Resource mechanisms

- Creation of participatory stakeholder/joint problem-solving workshops prior to and during implementation processes
- Creation of ad hoc task forces and cross-ministerial commissions with specific implementation tasks

Analytical aids

- Management Information Systems
- Developing a change mechanism plan that recognizes importance of early wins and stability in guiding coalition

Task: Capacity Building and Operations

Implementation tasks

- Building legitimacy by raising awareness of need for reform
- Develop convening authority: a forum in which decision-making may proceed
- Building constituencies

Resource/Mechanisms

- Create new forums for policy discussion, such as policy dialogue workshop, public-private forums; and task forces
- Identify, lobby and mobilize potential reform champions and stakeholders

Analytical aids

- Conduct stakeholder analysis
  - Clarify leadership/coordination function needed (reducing confusion, conflict)

Task: Legitimation and consensus building

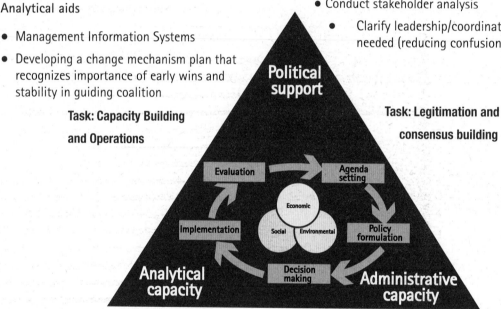

Task: Policy design and operational planning

Implementation tasks

- Designing coherent, integrated interventions
- Identification and mobilization of resources from various sources
- Detailing operational plans

Resources/Mechanisms

- Identify and obtain seed and bridge financing from internal/external sources

- Negotiation with finance and budget authorities for resources

Analytical aids

- Logical framework analysis, result-based planning
- Feasability assessment via scenario planning and forward/backward planning

take on a slightly different set of tasks, or a non-governmental or private company via delegation or contracting. Policy managers should develop and use accountability and management systems when allocating tasks. These systems need to be underpinned by an agreement on performance indicators, effective information systems that reliably update stakeholders and managers on the state of targeted outputs, and the mobilization of sufficient incentives and disincentives at the disposal of policy managers or higher authorities to motivate an acceptably high level of implementation effort.

Yet accountability can only partly rely on such formal measures; it is well known that many developing countries are often weak in such areas. Instead, the capacity to implement integrated policies will also rely on the density of relationships – the "social capital" – among local actors such as NGOs, communities, local government coordinators, and line agencies.[51]

6.3 Mobilize resources proactively

Ultimately public policies and their component programmes and plans must be integrated into normal budget cycles and operations. Before this can happen, managers of such initiatives will have to be creative and entrepreneurial in identifying sources of the resources necessary to get initial efforts off the ground.

Resources necessary and sufficient for effective implementation rarely "report for duty" simply because agreement has been reached on some policy objectives. More often, they must be mobilized from a variety of sources in a process that can determine to a large extent how effective and timely implementation proceeds. Policy managers and implementers are advised to view resource mobilization as a constant challenge rather than a one-off task.

This process is likely to be iterative. An initial challenge is the identification of seed or "bridge" financing and allocations of personnel that can enable integrated policies to get off the ground and initial activities to begin. To secure such initial financing often requires a hefty degree of negotiation with a range of actors, including government budget authorities and potential external partners. In the longer term, securing stable sources of fiscal and other necessary resources often comes from initial

---

> ### Box 6.2: Results Based Management (RBM)
>
> RBM is an approach to systematically planning for implementation. It has been increasingly promoted among multi-lateral development agencies and some developing country administrations. The Asian Development Bank, one of the foremost proponents of RBM, defines it as "the way an organization is motivated and applies processes and resources to achieve targeted results". Four components are noted: a) specified results that are measurable, monitorable and relevant; b) resources that are adequate for achieving the targeted results; c) organizational arrangements that ensure authority and responsibilities are aligned with results and resources; d) processes for planning, monitoring, communicating and resource release that enable the organization to convert resources into the desired results.
>
> Regardless of whether the technical approaches outlined under different RBM manuals are followed, policy managers will need to plan for the four dimensions quoted above, since they will often be under great pressure to demonstrate early results to half-hearted, skeptical stakeholders.
>
> Source: Asian Development Bank (2007) "Results Based Management Explained".
> http://www.adb.org/projects/rbm/about.asp

demonstrations of success coupled with more official, legally grounded framework for IP.

6.4 Managing stakeholder dynamics

Perhaps the most fundamental advice that can be offered regarding implementation is as follows: be aware of, and prepared for, the stakeholder dynamics. Implementation of integrated policies is fundamentally a challenge of coordination. And while coordination has a number of requirements – among them the capacity elements discussed below – the prerequisite for dealing effectively with any of them is a thorough understanding of the stakeholder environment.

Stakeholder analysis – one of the "building blocks" – serves as an analytical aid in this context and it could or should be conducted much earlier in the policy cycle.

It is discussed in this chapter because stakeholder dynamics is the most decisive factor affecting the success and failure of policy implementation.

There are a wide variety of formats and variations on stakeholder analysis, but they share some features: the delineation of all actors potentially concerned by, interested in, important to, or having any power over the policy being initiated. This is followed by consideration of their interests, level of organization, resources and capacities, and options for action. This information can be visually arrayed in a number of formats, in ways that help identify entry points for learning from, winning the support or overcoming the opposition of different stakeholders.

Mapping the level of power of participants leads to another consideration. Many policies will in some way affect stakeholders and communities that are relatively powerless and marginalized. Such stakeholders often have little means to make their concerns and priorities known to powerful actors. In the interest of equity and ultimately implementation effectiveness, policy managers should strengthen vulnerable stakeholders' ability to voice their interests and inform the direction of policymaking and implementation; civil society groups could play a pivotal role in this regard. The information gathering and communication to the public should be organized early in the process. Such strengthening of the "demand side" of IP needs to go together with an appreciation of the ways powerful actors can "capture" policymaking for their own benefit. This is particularly important where procedural safeguards, transparency levels, and grassroots democracy are weak in a particular society.

Illustration: Implementing the Kyoto Protocol in the European Union

In March of 2005 the Kyoto Protocol came into force. Governments are responsible for implementing protocols they have signed up to. Of all signatory countries, those in the EU are known as the most active in implementation. Even before the Protocol took effect, in January 2005, the EU had already started operationalizing the European Union Green House Gas Emission Trading Scheme (EU ETS). The EU considered implementation challenges early on. In 2003, for example, it already started designing the ETS scheme including the establishment of a Central Administrator and a registries' system to keep track of

transactions in emission trading. Stakeholder dynamics was also managed carefully by, for example, issuing emission units to industries at no charge rather than through auction; this has helped reduce the opposition from affected groups to the implementation of the ETS. In early 2009, the European Union announced that its goal was to link up the EU Emissions Trading System with the cap-and-trade systems being developed in other industrialized countries to form an OECD-wide international carbon market by 2015.

Further Reading

Brinkerhoff, D.W. and Crosby, B.L. (2002) *Managing Policy Reform: Concepts and tools for Decision-Makers in Developing and Transition Countries.* Bloomfield, CT: Kumarian Press.

Crosby, B.L. (1996) Policy implementation: The organizational challenge. *World Development* 24(9):1403-1415.

OECD (2001) "Policies to Enhance Sustainable Development", Meeting of the OECD Council at Ministerial Level, 2001, Paris: OECD.

Rondinelli, D.A. (1993) *Development Projects as Policy Experiments: An Adaptive Approach to Development Administration.* London: Routledge.

Uphoff, N., Esman, M.J., and Krishna, A. (1998) *Reasons for Success: Learning from Instructive Experiences in Rural Development.* Bloomfield, CT: Kumarian Press.

World Bank (2002) *World Development Report 2002: Building Institutions for Markets.* New York: Oxford University Press.

References

47. Teall, C. (2004). *Multilateral Environmental Agreements and the Compliance Continuum.* Retrieved March 2009 from the Georgetown International Environmental Law Review: http://findarticles.com/p/articles/mi_qa3970/is_200404/ai_n9406137

48. Rondinelli, 1993

49. Brinkerhoff and Crosby, 2002, p. 25

50. Several of these are mentioned in various forms in Brinkerhoff and Crosby, 2002.

51. Brown and Ashman, 1996

7. Evaluation

Integrated evaluation refers to the effort to monitor and determine how a policy has fared during implementation from an SD perspective. It examines the means employed, the objectives served, and the effects caused in practice. The results and recommendations from evaluation are fed back into further rounds of policymaking, as in the case of the regular review of the Poverty Reduction Strategy Papers (PRSPs) in low-income countries. In many cases, some aspects of evaluation such as data collection are also conducted during earlier stages of policymaking and the results can feed into the refinement of policy design, decision, and implementation.

Evaluation is expected to contribute to IP by: 1) synthesizing what is known about a problem, its proposed remedy, and the ESE effects from implementing the remedy, in order to facilitate policy learning; 2) demystifying conventional wisdom or popular myths related to the problem, its solutions,

---

Evaluation – Key points

Specifying the type, scope, and criteria of evaluation

- Ensure that ESE criteria and indicators are included – apart from the policy objectives – for guiding monitoring and evaluation.

- Define the scope for evaluation based on the amount of information available, the budget, and what is to be done with the findings from evaluation.

- Use the same ESE criteria and indicators as well as the policy objectives established in earlier stages of policymaking to be consistent.

Collecting data and isolating policy effects

- Take the scope of evaluation as the starting point for monitoring efforts and collect related data using methods, data systems, and analytical units appropriate for evaluative analysis.

- Engage statistical and analytical agencies from the start of a policy process.

- Avoid bias in data collection and isolate the effects of the policy from the effects of other forces to the extent possible.

Conducting Participatory Monitoring and Evaluation (PME)

- Engage stakeholders in monitoring or evaluation so that they share control over the content, the process, and the results of the PME activity.

- Engage stakeholders in identifying or taking corrective actions.

Ensuring policy learning

- Develop political will and maturity to use evaluation results and stimulate public demand for policy learning.

- Encourage a flexible and adaptive approach to policymaking, adjust policy implementation to reflect changing circumstances and lessons revealed from evaluation.

- Clarify, specify, and publicize government intentions for the policy, the evaluation criteria and indicators, and their justification.

- Establish and maintain links between the evaluation agency and other policy participants to ensure that lessons from evaluation will indeed feed into further policy processes.

and the effects of the solutions; 3) developing new information about policy effectiveness, such as the extent to which expected policy results have been achieved and the range and magnitude of unintended effects, in order to give early warning; and 4) explaining to all policy participants the implications of new information derived through evaluation, which may call for re-planning at the operational level.

This chapter describes how to determine the actual effects of an implemented policy, not only on the objectives established for the respective policy, but also the ESE dimensions of SD. It focuses on four steps:
1) specifying the type, scope, and criteria of evaluation;
2) collecting data and isolating policy effects;
3) conducting PME; and 4) ensuring policy learning.

7.1 Specifying the type, scope, and criteria of evaluation

There exist different, potentially related types of evaluation. Government policy managers and other participants involved in evaluation need to be certain which type is of primary interest. Some are initiated by governments, others by non-governmental actors. Both may conduct evaluations themselves or contract professional evaluators to perform evaluation tasks. Different types of evaluation may differ significantly in their level of formality and technical sophistication, the depth of data collection and analysis, and the conclusions that can be drawn. Further complicating evaluation is the fact that in most societies different actors can undertake different forms of evaluation simultaneously for the same policy and the results of these multiple efforts can complement or contradict each other, affecting the lessons that may be drawn. Box 7.1 describes some commons types of evaluation.

Of these various types of evaluation currently characterized by policy scientists, what is called "adequacy of performance evaluation" is perhaps the most pertinent to IP. In addition to evaluating a policy

---

Box 7.1: Types of Policy Evaluation

- **Effort (input) evaluation** is an attempt to measure the quantity of inputs – personnel, office space, communication, transportation, and so on—all of which are calculated in terms of the monetary costs they involve. The purpose of this type of evaluation is to establish a baseline of data that can be used for further evaluations of the efficiency or quality of public service delivery.

- **Performance (output) evaluation** examines outputs - such as the number of hospital beds, the number of schools, and the number of patients seen or children taught - rather than inputs. The aim of performance evaluation is to determine what the policy is producing, sometimes regardless of the stated objectives. This type of evaluation produces benchmark or performance data that are used as inputs into the more comprehensive and intensive evaluations mentioned below.

- **Process evaluation** examines the organizational methods including rules and operating procedures that are used to deliver policy components. The objective is usually to see if a process can be streamlined and made more efficient.

- **Efficiency evaluation** attempts to assess the costs of a programme and judge if the same amount and quality of outputs could be achieved at a lower cost. Input and output evaluations are the building blocks of this form of evaluation.

- **Evaluation of the policy assessment** may be conducted to learn lessons on the various aspects of assessment such as the stakeholders involved, analyses conducted, the communication of the assessment results, the influence on decision-making, etc.

- **Adequacy of performance evaluation** (also known as effectiveness evaluation) compares the performance of a given policy to its intended objectives to determine whether the policy is meeting its objectives and whether the objectives need to be adjusted in the light of the policy's accomplishments. For integrated policy evaluation, however, ESE criteria agreed at the decision-making stage should also be included as the basis for evaluation.

against its objectives, however, additional ESE criteria need be included for integrated policy evaluation, which is the focus of this chapter.

Policy managers, together with those who will perform evaluation tasks, also need to determine the scope of integrated evaluation. At a general level the scope should be guided by what is required of integrated evaluation, i.e. comparing policy performance to the agreed policy objectives and ESE criteria. At the operational level, the scope of evaluation needs to be defined based on the amount of information available for evaluative analysis and what is to be done with the findings from evaluation.

Possible conclusions of evaluation range from maintaining all aspects of an existing policy to changing the policy substance and process, and rarely, terminating the policy. Accordingly, evaluation can involve merely reviewing – through timely monitoring – how established policy components are doing and whether the assumptions underlining the policy and its components appear to be correct. Or it can aid in deciding whether or how the policy initiative should be modified, defending the proponent's ideas, and recording achievements for succeeding policy debates, deliberations, and arguments. For example, one of the things that may be made clear is whether the policy objectives established at the policy formulation stage are "operationalizable" on the ground and whether those objectives should be reformulated.

Evaluation criteria provide standards by which policy outcomes can be evaluated.[52] They enable evaluation activities to focus on the aspects of policy outcomes that are valued most by the society. Policy outcomes are often multi-faceted, and different judgments can be made depending on which aspects of policy outcomes are emphasized. For example, the success of a policy designed to reduce school drop-out rates may be evaluated by the changes in school drop-out rates before and after the implementation of the policy, as well as related indicators such as changes in household income levels (due to changes in family labour supply as children stop helping in the filed or factories).

To be consistent, evaluators should use the same criteria and indicators established for comparing policy options during the decision-making stage.

These criteria and indicators should cover the ESE concerns as well as the primary objectives to be achieved by the policy. This assumes, however, that the ESE concerns have indeed been integrated in the earlier stages of the policy process. This may not be the case in practice. There are many cases, however, where the integration has not taken place earlier in the policy process or where ESE concerns have only been partially addressed. In such cases, achieving integrated policy evaluation requires ESE criteria and indicators to be established and applied anew. This retroactive, or ex-post approach is most valuable for generating general lessons for future policy development, but has limited influence on the orientation of the policy being implemented. This is exactly why IP is promoted as an effort to internalize ESE considerations within a policy process from the very beginning.

7.2 Collecting data and isolating policy effects

Integrated policy evaluation has a particularly strong demand for data on the various effects that have been generated from policy implementation. Only by using such data can the evaluator conduct an analysis to determine whether the observed effects are in line with the policy objectives and the ESE criteria and indicators. Monitoring of policy performance, which collects data and information, therefore, is an indispensable component of the policy evaluation stage. The monitoring agency – whether the evaluating agency itself or another designated agency – takes the scope of evaluation as a starting point, collects the required data, and feeds the results into evaluative analysis.

There are two major types of data collection methods with different cost and time implications: primary and secondary. Primary data are collected directly by the organization responsible for evaluation, which tends to take more time and cost more. Secondary data are already collected by other organizations for purposes other than the evaluation concerned, which is less expensive. Examples of secondary data include national census, financial market data, or demographic health survey data. Box 7.3 describes a sub-category of data collection methods.

Before setting out to collect data, however, monitoring and evaluating agencies should establish or adopt data systems and analytical units. For example, for agriculture policy's effects on biodiversity, there are World Conservation Union (IUCN) red-list of endangered species, UNEP-World Conservation Monitoring Centre (WCMC) protected areas database, and a lot of Geographic Information System datasets owned by space agencies. As far as analytical units are concerned, the biodiversity effects of agriculture policy can be analysed in terms of the area of habitats altered or population of selected species threatened. These questions are preferably dealt with when defining the criteria and indicators at the decision-making stage.

Thus, working with statistical and analytical agencies in government at the outset of a policy process is much more time and resource effective, for example, than trying to "retro-fit" existing data sources after-the-fact. And, in many cases, the only

way to effectively assess the impacts of a policy intervention is to have baseline data before the policy change, which can be compared to the same data collected after the policy and its component programmes and plans have been put into effect. That is, in many cases retroactively attempting to reconstruct a policy baseline may be impossible.

In designing data-gathering activities, policy managers, monitoring agents, and evaluators should anticipate the kind of results that can occur from both official and unofficial policy evaluation. Policy evaluation should be designed in a way to ensure policy "judges" are provided with enough good information to allow for reasonably intelligent, defensible, and replicable assessments of ongoing policy processes and outcomes. Policy managers, in particular, must ensure that accurate and unbiased information is available to concerned individuals,

---

Box 7.2: Data Collection Methods in Policy Evaluation

■ **Sample surveys:** Sample surveys provide comprehensive and vital information about the target population. Done properly, sample surveys lead to conclusions about the entire population based on trends and patterns of change within the representative sample.

■ **Case studies:** As a good complement to methods involving larger samples such as surveys, case studies document the life story or sequence of events over time related to a person, location, household, or organization to obtain insight into the impacts of a policy.

■ **Key informant interviews:** One-on-one talk about a specific topic or issue with an individual recognized or designated as a community or institutional leader. The aim is to learn the key person's views and perceptions of the policy, its process, the related political setting.

■ **Focus group discussions:** Focus groups elicit a multiplicity of views within a group context in a way that individual interviews cannot (for example, in statistical surveys), or to gather local terminology or beliefs for research purposes. Focus group discussions can be used as an individual monitoring activity or as a complement to other methods, especially for triangulation and validity checking.

■ **Community group interviews:** Series of set questions and facilitated discussion in an interview meeting open to all community members used to gather views and feedback of beneficiaries and other stakeholders to be used by decision-makers and to disseminate information to the community.

■ **Direct observation:** Detailed observation of what is seen or heard on the ground where a policy is expected to take effect. Very useful as a means to report on behaviours, actions, and processes, for example, a change in behaviour of extension workers toward ethnic minorities as a result of a project training activity.

Adapted from: World Bank: Social and Environmental Sustainability of Agriculture and Rural Development Investments: A Monitoring and Evaluation Toolkit

---

Table 7.1: Evaluation Design for Isolating Net Outcomes from Gross Outcomes

Type	Description
Design 1: Randomized controlled trials	A randomized controlled trial establishes the net impact of a policy by exposing a group of people to the policy intervention in question (the experimental group) whilst withholding the policy to a comparison group (the control group). The allocation of people or units to the experimental and control group is undertaken on a randomized basis.
Design 2: Before/after comparison	It takes a single sample of the population and exposes it to a policy or programme initiative, and the net effect size is measured in terms of the difference in the outcome of interest before and after the intervention is introduced.
Design 3: Matched comparison	In this design, an experimental group is exposed to a policy whilst a closely matched control group does not receive the policy in question.

groups, and organizations. With this goal in mind, they should ensure that policymaking is transparent and accountable in order to discourage misperceptions about the role and intentions of government in implementing policies.

In this regard, it is important for evaluators to distinguish between gross outcomes and net outcomes of a policy to the extent possible.[53, 54] Gross outcomes consist of all observed changes in an outcome measure for the policy, and net outcomes are those effects that can be reasonably attributed to the policy. The effects of other policies and events also include cumulative effects, which may be difficult to attribute to any causes. The relationship between gross outcomes and net outcomes can be expressed as:

Gross outcome={net outcome}+{effects of other policies}+{effects of other events }.

Table 7.1 lists three commonly used evaluation designs in isolating the net outcome from gross outcome. While some designs are more likely to produce more credible estimates of policy outcomes than others, in practice it is difficult or impossible to adopt the "best" evaluation design due to time and resource constraints. The evaluators should instead choose the best possible design by taking into consideration the importance of the policy, the practicality of evaluation designs, and the probability of producing useful and credible results.

7.3 Conducting Participatory Monitoring and Evaluation (PME)

PME is a process through which stakeholders at various levels engage in monitoring or evaluating a particular project, programme, or policy, share control over the content, the process, and the results of the PME activity, and engage in identifying or taking corrective actions. It focuses on the active engagement (with capacity building elements) of primary stakeholders to evaluate government efforts and outputs. Table 7.2 compares the conventional and participatory approaches to evaluation.

Using formal consultations with members of affected public or other stakeholders is becoming a common practice. There are many mechanisms for such consultations, which policy managers should embrace. These include setting up forums for public hearings and establishing special consultative committees, task forces, and inquiries for evaluative purposes. These can range from small meetings of less than a dozen participants lasting several minutes to multi-million dollar inquiries that hear thousands of individual briefs and can take years to complete. In many societies, political evaluation of government action is built into the system, in the form, for example, of congressional or parliamentary oversight committees or mandated administrative review processes. While in some countries these tend to occur on a regular basis, in others the

Table 7.2: Conventional and Participatory Modes of Evaluation

	Conventional	**Participatory**
Who plans and manages the process?	Policy managers, outside experts	Affected groups, policy implementers, as well as policy managers
Role of primary stakeholders	Provide information only	Collect and analyse data and information, share findings, and take actions
How success is measured?	Externally defined, mainly quantitative indicators	Internally defined indicators, more qualitative indicator
Approach	Pre-determined, standardized	Adaptive

process may be less routine, and operate on a more ad hoc basis.

7.4 Ensuring policy learning

The designation of a policy as a success or failure is often a semantic tool used in public debates and policy contestations to seek political advantage. Policy evaluation involves attributing blame and credit for government activities, which can have electoral and other political consequences for policy actors, making it an unavoidably political process. These political challenges and other challenges in policy evaluation are described in Box 7.3.

To overcome purely subjective or politically-motivated evaluations, policy managers and evaluators promote evaluation as an approach to policy learning. [55] They can develop political will and maturity to use evaluation results and stimulate

---

Box 7.3: Challenges in Policy Evaluation

■ **Political time and evaluation time.** It takes time to evaluate policy adequantely, but the political world moves at faster pace. As a result, policy-makers and other key stakeholders are often impatient and demand quick evaluation.

■ **Political motives for evaluation.** Evaluation is often employed in a biased and self-interested manner for political reason. For example, evaluation may be conducted to disguise or conceal a situation feared to show the government in a poor light, and sometimes the evaluation is designed to gain partisan political advantage or reinforce pre-set ideological postulates instead of to improve policymaking.

■ **Lack of absorptive capacity.** A high level of absorptive capacity is required if the lessons of evaluations are to be properly assimilated, but the extent to which such capacity exists in government varies greatly from jurisdiction to jurisdiction, and from sector to sector or issue to issue.

■ **Lack of information.** Evaluation requires the collection of precise information on policy performance and impacts, and its compilation in a standardized fashion in order to allow comparisons of costs and outcomes over time and across policy sectors. Information gathering and management systems in themselves are quite technical and increasingly sophisticated.

■ **Lack of expertise.** The evaluation of integrated policies, in view of the inherent complexities, often requries technical expertise that is often not readily available in many countries.

public demand for policy learning. They can also encourage building in a flexible and adaptive approach to policy design. Box 7.4 describes major types of policy learning.[56]

In addition, policy managers, monitoring agencies, and evaluators can request that government intentions be clarified, made consistent, and publicized in various fora such as agency or legislative websites and annual reports as well as media releases and educational materials. They can, at the same time, request that criteria for determining success and failure are clearly specified and their rationales justified and adhered to by government spokespersons. And they can continually monitor changing circumstances and alter some aspects of policies as these circumstances unfold. That is, they should not insist or pretend that governments are infallible or omniscient but rather promote as much as possible the notion that governments are learning organizations and ensure that lessons are indeed learned and fed back into further policy processes.

Finally, policy managers should establish links between the evaluating organization and its environment, and within a governmental organization, between an evaluating agency and new and existing stores of information.[57] Enhancing the organizational capacity of the state agencies involved in IP is critical to ensure that learning, of any kind, results from evaluation. Policy managers involved in IP, therefore, must concern themselves with establishing and maintaining these links.

Illustration: Evaluating the implementation of the Kyoto Protocol

Each year the 192 countries that are party to the UNFCCC hold a Conference of Parties (COP). The COP forms the governing body of the UNFCCC and oversees the implementation of the Kyoto Protocol. In 2005, the annual COP was supplemented with a meeting of the parties to the Kyoto Protocol (CMP or COP/MOP), and this has remained the case since. From 1995 to 2008, a total of 14 annual COPs were held, the latest in Poznan, Poland, in December 2008. COP's responsibilities include monitoring, enforcing compliance, and evaluation of Annex I countries' implementation of their commitments. The evaluation focuses on two major factors: 1) whether Parties

---

Box 7.4: Four types of policy learning

Social learning is the most general and significant type of learning which policy managers can promote and to which they must react. It involves fundamental shifts in public attitudes and perceptions of social problems and policy issues and involves different types of actors, both inside and outside of governments and existing policy subsystems.

Lesson-drawing is a more limited, means-oriented, type of learning. It involves a variety of actors drawing lessons from their own experiences and the experiences of others in implementing existing policies.

Policy-oriented learning is a more restricted type of learning that involves the clarification of existing goals and policy beliefs based on experiences gained from evaluations of existing policies. It is the most common type of learning to emerge from typical policy evaluation activities.

Government learning is the most restricted type of learning. It involves reviews of policy and programme behaviour by existing actors and tends to be means-oriented at best. Its impact and consequences are generally limited to improvement of the means by which policies are implemented and administered.

---

follow the Protocol's rulebook and comply with their commitments; and 2) whether the emissions data used to assess compliance is reliable.

To enable effective evaluation, the Kyoto Protocol included a set of monitoring and compliance procedures to enforce the Protocol's rules, address any compliance problems, and avoid any error in calculating emissions data and accounting for transactions under the three Kyoto mechanisms – emissions trading, clean development mechanism and joint implementation. Article 5 of the Kyoto Protocol, for example, commits Annex I Parties to having in place, no later than 2007, national systems for the estimation of greenhouse gas emissions by sources and removals by sinks. Article 7 requires Annex I

Parties to submit annual greenhouse gas inventories, as well as national communications, at regular intervals, both including supplementary information to demonstrate compliance with the Protocol. Article 8 states that expert review teams will review the inventories as well as the national communications submitted by Annex I Parties. In addition, the Kyoto Protocol states that guidelines for national systems, adjustments, the preparation of inventories and national communications, as well as for the conduct of expert reviews should be regularly reviewed thereby providing the basis for policy learning.

The parties to the UNFCCC agreed at COP13 in Bali in December 2007 that negotiations on a future agreement have to be concluded at COP15 in Copenhagen. This decision was made based on the recommendation of the UN Intergovernmental Panel on Climate Change on the need for swift action to urgently fight climate change. And also the recognition that 2009 will be one of the last chances for an agreement if it is to be approved and ratified prior to the expiry of the commitments set in the Kyoto Protocol in 2012.

Further Reading

Chelimsky, E. (1995). New Dimensions in Evaluation. Evaluation and Development: Proceedings of the World bank Conference on Evaluation and Development. W. Bank, International Bank for Reconstruction and Development: 3-14.

Davidson, E. J. (2005). Evaluation Methodology Basics. Sage, Thousand Oaks.

Hellstern, G.-M. (1986). Assessing Evaluation Research. Guidance, Control, and Evaluation in the Public Sector. F.-X. Kaufman, G. Majone and V. Ostrom. Berlin, Walter de Gruyter: 279-312.

Langbein, L. and C. L. Felbinger (2006). Public Programme Evaluation: A Statistical Guide. Armonk, M.E. Sharpe.

Rossi, P. H., M. W. Lipsey, et al. (2004). Evaluation: A Systematic Approach. Thousand Oaks, Sage.

Stufflebeam, D. L. (2001). "Evaluation Models." New Directions for Evaluation 89: 7-98.

References

52. Swiss, J. E. (1991). Public Management Systems: Monitoring and Managing Government Performance. Upper Saddle River, N.J., Prentice Hall.

53. Rossi and Freeman, 1993

54. McLaughlin, M. W. (1985). Implementation Realities and Evaluation Design. *Social Science and Social Policy*. R. L. Shotland and M. M. Mark, Beverly Hills: Sage: 96-120.

55. Sanderson, I. (2002). "Evaluation, Policy Learning and Evidence-Based Policy Making." *Public Administration* 80(1): 1-22.

56. Davidson, E. J. (2005). *Evaluation Methodology Basics.* Sage, Thousand Oaks.

57. Mitchell, R. and S. Nicholas (2006). "Knowledge Creation Through Boundary-Spanning." *Knowledge Management Research and Practice* 4: 310-318.

8. Conclusion

This manual has introduced an integrated approach to public policymaking. It has argued that the demand for such an approach has come from a number of international processes, including the MDGs, WSSD, MA, and MEAs. It has acknowledged that many organizations have responded to the call for integrated policymaking by developing various sustainability-oriented policy assessment initiatives. It has explained that IP is another response to the need for proactive integration of SD considerations into policymaking.

The manual has offered a framework for applying the IP approach. Integration is interpreted at three levels. First, the ESE dimensions of SD must be integrated and considered jointly in relation to a policy issue and its solutions. Second, the ESE considerations must be factored into each stage of the policy process. Third, IP must bring political, administrative, and financial constraints into account.

Specifically, at the agenda-setting stage, a problem of public concern should be defined in relation to a society's SD context, including priorities, risks and opportunities, as well as to the concerns of other sectors and groups that may affect the problem and its resolution. During policy formulation, the root-cause analysis of the problem should find out the critical ESE factors and their inter-linkages in causing the problem and when screening policy options, the political, administrative, and financial feasibility should be considered. In the decision-making stage, projected implications of policy options related to ESE criteria and indicators should serve as the basis for deciding which policy option should be selected. In implementation, the challenge is to ensure that policy interventions, which have supposedly integrated ESE consideration, do actually take place on the ground. When it comes to evaluation, policy performance is examined against both the established policy objectives and the ESE criteria/indicators.

In all of these activities, individual policy participants, including policy managers, initiators, formulators, decision-makers, implementers, monitoring agents, evaluators, and many other actors involved in the policy process – are expected to perform their roles according to the requirements of IP.

Conclusion – Key points

- Recognize that this manual, on its own, is inadequate to persuade policymakers and other participants to adopt IP

- Need to demonstrate the risks of unsustainable development and opportunities from seeking synergies among ESE dimensions of SD in order to create a genuine appreciation of the need for an integrated approach to policymaking

- Organize or reinvigorate an SD "policy community" to review related national frameworks and institutional arrangements and propose improvements focusing on SD criteria and indicators as well as the effectiveness of related institutions

- Invest in sustainability-related statistical capacities in developing countries with a focus on having an adequate number of qualified statisticians, acquiring and maintaining related data systems, and sustaining the regular data collection and reporting operations

- Provide long-term as well as short-term training to create a critical mass of qualified policy analysts who can potentially assume the roles of policy managers, initiators, formulators, decision-makers, implementers, monitoring agents, and evaluators in support of IP

This assumes, however, that all these actors are already convinced of the value of IP and are already motivated to apply this approach. Clearly, this is a generous assumption. This manual may guide efforts in pursuing IP, but on its own it is not enough to persuade policy participants to adopt such an approach.

To gear public policies towards SD requires much more than a manual or hundreds of manuals. It requires a genuine conviction of the need for SD on the part of governments and citizens. This, in turn, needs to come from a true appreciation of the risks from pursuing particular societal objectives at the expense of other objectives and the opportunities from seeking synergies that exist among a society's ESE imperatives. Analysts can demonstrate these risks and opportunities through case studies. Advocacy groups and media can play an important role in communicating these risks and opportunities.

But even when individuals in the government and society are convinced of the need for SD and willing to apply IP, they face tremendous institutional and capacity constraints, some of which have been identified in the preceding chapters. The rest of this chapter focuses on how to strengthen institutions and capacities to ease the transition towards IP. It focuses on four aspects: 1) reviewing the current status of the SD discussion at the national level; 2) improving the national SD frameworks and related institutional arrangements based on the results of the review; 3) systematically investing in statistical capacity to support sustainability-related analytical work; and 4) provide training in IP to cultivate a critical mass of policy analysts at the national level that could potentially assume the roles of policy managers, initiators, formulators, evaluators, etc. as described in this manual.

8.1 Reviewing the status of SD discussions

Most governments have made commitments to SD in one form or another. Many of them have also developed related policies, programmes, plans, procedures, criteria, and indicators, mostly at a general level. A few countries have established institutions to be in charge of SD issues, typically dominated by environmental issues. These general expressions of commitments to SD, however, are often not matched by the way in which national budgets

are allocated.[58] This has invited questions on the seriousness of the commitments.

It will, therefore, be useful to review the SD discussions at the country level. The purpose is to ascertain how the concept of SD is understood by the government and different segments of society, whether the various policy, programmes, plans, procedures, criteria, and indicators under the SD banner reflect a common understanding domestically and internationally, as well as the functions and effectiveness of related institutional arrangements. This type of review is important for IP, which requires the framing of policy issues in relation to a society's SD context, the use of ESE criteria and indicators to guide decisions and evaluation, and the coordination among sectors and agencies.

Various actors can initiate and sponsor such reviews. Governments and domestic groups, for example, may want to take stock of national understanding and practice related to SD. External organizations promoting SD may also sponsor such reviews. The OECD, for example, has conducted such reviews in its member states and in some partner countries. This effort could be expanded to cover other countries, but national ownership of such reviews is the key to ensuring their usefulness.

8.2 Improving national SD frameworks and institutional arrangements

Based on the review mentioned above, government officials in charge of SD together with other actors may want to consider whether existing SD frameworks and institutional arrangements may require adjustment. For example, if the concept of SD as practiced reflects an excessive emphasis on sustaining economic growth to the disadvantage of social equity and environmental integrity, a more balanced approach may need to be introduced and related criteria and indicators developed. If an agency in charge of SD does not have the convening power to bring line agencies together, it may also call for alternative arrangements.

As far as having supportive institutions for IP is concerned, major efforts are often needed to establish SD criteria and indicators. A number of inter-governmental bodies have spent many years to develop such criteria and indicators, but translating them into the national level remains a challenge. These criteria and indicators are sometimes not explicitly publicized. Where they are, they tend to stay at a general level, defying any effort to measure them. In a few cases where specific national level SD criteria and indicators do exist, they may not be translated into the sector level. In this regard, it may also be noted that in most countries the allocation of public budgets is typically not tied to any SD criteria and indicators.

Making improvements along these lines, however, is likely to encounter the very same constraints that IP does, i.e. the political, administrative, and analytical factors that may pose as barriers. Thus, anyone who would like to initiate the SD review and propose improvements may want to proceed with a modest pace. Organizing or reinvigorating a SD "policy community" that consists of government officials, technical experts, journalists, and civil society representatives may be the first step needed to initiate the review and discuss improvements. Indeed, it is a policy process in its own right.

8.3 Investing in SD-related statistical capacity

A chronic constraint experienced by most countries in operationalizing SD (including the uptake of IP) is the lack of related data and statistics, especially on the social and environmental dimensions of sustainability. Although one may want to explore the ESE root causes of a policy issue and use ESE criteria and indicators to guide decision and evaluation, if regular data collection for important indicators is difficult, then IP is unlikely to go very far. In many sustainability-oriented assessments, for example, the choice of indicators tends to be ad hoc and mostly qualitative, reflecting a serious lack of data to support integrated analysis.

This problem is especially acute in developing countries whose statistical agencies are typically under-budgeted relative to the role they are expected to play for supporting good policy analysis. IP imposes additional requirements in terms of the range and type of data to be collected. For these agencies to meet the needs of IP, they would require support in recruiting and retaining an adequate number of trained statistical personnel, acquiring and maintaining data systems that are internationally comparable, and sustaining data collection and

reporting operations on a regular basis. All of these require investments by the public sector.

External agencies could help developing countries strengthen their SD-related statistical capacity through direct budget support. In addition, inter-governmental statistical organizations should establish long-term programmes to provide related training to statistical professionals in these countries. Various ongoing statistical training activities do exist, but they tend to be run along sectoral lines. It is suggested that broad ESE dimensions of SD be incorporated into existing statistical training curriculums, especially in the short term when the same statisticians in developing countries are likely to be responsible for a wide range of statistical tasks.

8.4 Provide training on IP

IP involves many actors: policy managers, initiators, formulators, decision-makers, implementers, monitoring agents, evaluators, and others, who may have overlapping functions (i.e. the same person may assume different roles). They are required to perform their roles according to the requirements of IP. For example, when framing an issue at the agenda-setting stage, they need to define issues in relation to a society's SD priorities. For decision-making, they need to project the implications of policy options against ESE criteria and indicators. Throughout the policy process, they need to engage and manage stakeholders. These responsibilities require skills that may be lacking in many countries.

As in the case of statistical capacity, there exist various training activities related to SD around the world. Training in IP may be tagged to these existing programmes. But care must be taken not to confuse the targeted audience. For example, IP has a number of overlaps with sustainability-related assessments especially at the decision-making stage as described in this manual where the ESE implications of policy options are projected. When tagging training activities to sustainability-related assessment training programmes, it is important to explain where things overlap and where things serve distinctive purposes.

For IP to be adopted as a routine approach to public policymaking, there is a need for a critical mass of high-quality policy analysts at the country level who could potentially play the roles of policy managers, initiators, formulators, decision-makers, implementers, monitoring agents, and evaluators. This requires systematic in addition to ad hoc training and educational programmes in IP. A good starting place is the public policy or public management programmes that currently exist in many higher education institutions. Professors and deans in these programmes are encouraged to build elements of IP into existing courses. At the same time, public institutions and external agencies can sponsor short-term courses on IP in response to the growing demand for professionals able to perform the various functions in IP.

58. OECD NSDP review.

Glossary

Agenda setting: First stage of a policy cycle, in which policy initiators define the list of issues or problems (including potential opportunities) that will receive the governments' attention

Baseline: Also referred to as a "business as usual" scenario, describes what would happen to established indicators if there were no change in government decisions and if existing trends were to continue. The baseline is different from the 'status quo'. The baseline provides an essential reference point against which various other policy options can be compared.

Decision-making: The third stage in the policy cycle, where one selects a course of action or non-action among a small set of options identified at the policy formulation stage with a view towards implementation

Environmental Impact Assessment: A process, applied mainly at project level, to improve decision making and to ensure that development options under consideration are environmental and socially sound and sustainable. A subset of tools has emerged from EIA, including social impact assessment, cumulative effects assessment, environmental health impact assessment, risk assessment, biodiversity impact assessment and SEA. http://www.oecd.org/dataoecd/4/21/37353858.pdf

Integrated Assessment (IA): Generally refers to an assessment that crosses issues; spans scales of space and time; looks forward and back; and includes stakeholder perspectives. IA is an important precursor for adaptive management and governance. By connecting assessment with policy, information moves beyond pure science and becomes both salient and legitimate to decision-making processes. Inclusion of stakeholder perspectives ensures relevance, another criterion for sound assessment. http://www.iisd.org/measure/learning/assessment/

Implementation: The stage of the policy cycle where a selected option must be translated into action, probably the most difficult, demanding and critical stage in a policy process.

Millennium Ecosystem Assessment (MA): A series of global comprehensive studies, aiming to assess the consequences of ecosystem change for human well-being. The MA has involved the work of more than 1,360 experts worldwide. Their findings, contained in five technical volumes and six synthesis reports, provide a state-of-the-art scientific appraisal of the condition and trends in the world's ecosystems and the services they provide (such as clean water, food, forest products, flood control, and natural resources) and the options to restore, conserve or enhance the sustainable use of ecosystems. http://www.millenniumassessment.org/en/About.aspx

Multilateral Environmental Agreements (MEAs): A category of international agreements, that distinguish themselves by their focus on environmental issues, their creation of binding international law, and their inclusion of multiple countries. MEAs can be:

- Global or regional
- Appendix-driven or Annex-driven conventions
- Framework conventions

Each MEA require that countries develop specific implementation mechanisms and fulfill obligations involving reporting, training, public education, etc. http://www.unep.org/dec/docs/Guide%20for%20Negotiators%20of%20MEAs.pdf

Participatory Monitoring and Evaluation (PME): A process that emphasizes participation of the stakeholders in deciding how project progress should be measured and results acted on. It focuses on the active engagement (with capacity building elements) of primary stakeholders to evaluate government efforts and outputs. PME is potentially very empowering, as it puts local people in charge, helps develop their skills, shows that their views count, and provides an opportunity to share successes and learn from each other. Broadening the involvement of the various stakeholders in identifying and analysing change can create a clearer picture of what is really happening on the ground. http://www.idrc.ca/en/ev-26686-201-1-DO_TOPIC.html

Performance (output) evaluation: Is a type of policy evaluation that determines what the policy is producing (ex. number of units), sometimes regardless of the stated objectives. This type of evaluation produces benchmark or performance data that are used as inputs into the more comprehensive and intensive evaluations mentioned below.

Policy Cycle: A concept based on the understanding that, under normal circumstances, policy making is not linear, but a succession of stages and cycles without a clear starting point. One "standardized" version includes the following stages:

- Agenda setting (Problem identification)
- Policy formulation
- Decision making (Adoption)
- Implementation
- Evaluation

Policy evaluation (Integrated): Policy evaluation refers broadly to all the activities carried out by a range of state and societal actors at the last stage of the policy process. It involves the assessment of both the means being employed and the objectives being served, and of how a policy has actually fared in practice. Policy evaluation is a crucial step in policy development as the results are fed back directly into further rounds of policy-making, affecting future efforts at agenda-setting, policy formulation, decision-making and policy implementation, as well as future efforts at policy evaluation itself.

Policy formulation: Generally the second stage of a policy cycle, a process of generating policy options in response to a problem established during the agenda-setting stage.

Results Based Management (RBM): A life-cycle approach to management that integrates strategy, people, resources, processes and measurements to improve decision-making, transparency, and accountability, and to drive change. The approach focuses on achieving outcomes by getting the right design early in a process, implementing performance measurement, learning and changing, and reporting performance. Practically, RBM is an approach to systematically plan for implementation. http://www.acdi-cida.gc.ca/CIDAWEB/acdicida.nsf/En/NIC-31595014-KEF

Social learning: The most general and significant type of policy learning which policy managers can promote and to which they must react. It involves fundamental shifts in public attitudes and perceptions of social problems and policy issues and involves different types of actors, both inside and outside of governments and existing policy subsystems.

Sustainable Development (SD): The Brundtland Report defines SD as "development that meets the needs of the present without compromizing the ability of future generations to meet their own needs.". SD focuses on improving the quality of life for all of the Earth's citizens without increasing the use of natural resources beyond the capacity of the environment to supply them indefinitely. It requires an understanding that inaction has consequences and that we must find innovative ways to change institutional structures and influence individual behaviour. It is about taking action, changing policy and practice at all levels, from the individual to the international. http://www.unep.ch/etb/ publications/capacityBuilding/TrainingModule148.pdf

Strategic Environmental Assessment (SEA): Refers to a range of "analytical and participatory approaches that aim to integrate environmental considerations into policies, plans and programmes and evaluate the inter-linkages with economic and social considerations". SEA can be described as a family of approaches which use a variety of tools, rather than a single, fixed and prescriptive approach. A good SEA is adapted and tailor-made to the context in which it is applied. The emphasis is on the full integration of the environmental, social and economic factors into a holistic sustainability assessment.
http://www.oecd.org/dataoecd/4/21/37353858.pdf

World Summit on Sustainable Development (WSSD): The Johannesburg Summit 2002 – the World Summit on Sustainable Development – brought together tens of thousands of participants, including heads of state and government, national delegates and leaders from non-governmental organizations (NGOs), businesses and other major groups to focus the world's attention and direct action toward meeting difficult challenges, including improving people's lives and conserving natural resources in a world that is growing in population, with ever-increasing demands for food, water, shelter, sanitation, energy, health services and economic security.
http://www.un.org/jsummit/html/basic_info/basicinfo.html
http://www.un.org/jsummit/html/brochure/brochure12.pdf

Index